YOUR MIND IS YOUR
HOME

KAMRAN BEDI

hey,

Welcome to this wonderful book brought to you by That Guy's House Publishing.

At That Guy's House we believe in real and raw wellness books that inspire the reader from a place of authenticity and honesty.

This book has been carefully crafted by both the author and publisher with the intention that it will bring you a glimmer of hope, a rush of inspiration and sensation of inner peace.

It is our hope that you thoroughly enjoy this book and pass it onto friends who may also be in need of a glimpse into their own magnificence.

Have a wonderful day.

Love,

Sean Patrick

That Guy.

A Mind Of Its Own

You may or may not have noticed, that at certain angles, and in certain light, the colour of the cover of the book, changes. This teased me in so many ways upon receiving proof copies. Instead of summoning drastic changes at the 11th hour, we decided to keep the feature, which you may at times observe. Let this be a reminder to you that you will have bright days, grey days, happy moments, to times where you're challenged.

As you begin to progress through this book, allow yourself to observe the colours that present themselves to you, as you are reminded of the ability that you can now come to learn, for how to change and improve your mind.

Special thanks to Peter Watkins for designing the cover.

This book is dedicated to you the reader. May you now discover the peace, control and freedom that you yourself can implement to your own state of mind.

Table of Contents

Foreword by Katie Piper

Anyone who uses the internet and social media needs this book. OK let's change that - EVERYONE needs this book.

We've meticulously almost obsessively ensured that we have kept up to speed with the advances of technology, the latest apps, and social media trends. Ironically, the new and ever developing inventions that have been designed to make us more connected and 'social' than ever before, are potentially responsible in some ways for making us more disconnected. Instead of being 'social' we are in a lot of ways 'anti-social' where we are at times often left riddled with anxiety, depression and overactive thoughts like never before, don't you think?

Whilst concentrating on keeping ahead of new tech trends, what's trending and what everyone else online is sharing and 'doing', have we ensured the same safe-guarding of our own minds?

This book not only explores this question, but offers solutions, ways to cope, and essentially what we are looking for: freedom from our chaotic minds and sometimes overpowering and difficult thoughts. This may seem like a fantasy for many, to free their minds, however, it is possible through this book.

I've personally known Kamran for over a decade. Our friendship has seen us both go through some personal and difficult times, both where our minds have been our saviours. We've both learnt how to appreciate how strong the tool of our mind truly is. As my friend, confidant and now fellow author, I'm thrilled for you the reader, for you are about to embark on a personal journey with Kamran. As he shares his insights, knowledge, personal and professional experience with you, you will get the chance to experience his various methods for working on and improving the state of your mind.

When you've finished reading and working through this book, I want you to do one thing: pass it on. Pass it on to a friend, pass it on to a stranger, simply pass it on! We all seem to be coping so well from what we share on Facebook and Instagram, but do we really know the true depths of what someone is experiencing in their mind?

Introduction

Do you often find that you're stuck in your head watching your thoughts play out like scenes and mini-movies? Perhaps you even have a lot of 'chatter', internal dialogue and general noise playing through your mind? This never-ending screen and space that you watch and listen in on inside your head can at times be overly distracting and also overwhelming. You can very easily drift off into thoughts of your past or concerns for the future. Do you have any control over the actions of your mind? This personal and private space that only you know of and experience within your own head can drain your energy, fill you with worry and at times play out every worse-case scenario.

Imagine now, if the thoughts you were thinking were all projected out publicly on a news feed style forum, for the world to see. How would the thought of your private and personal inner world being reflected out in a futuristic *Black Mirror* style app for all to watch and see, affect you? You see, anyone can add a filter, choose a good angle, and portray the perfect image and ideal life in an Instagram or a social media post, but what's it really like living your life? Your ability to document the good, to share and parade your outer life publicly is all too easy, but how about the state of your mind? What about your true mental and emotional health, or what's really and honestly happening for you on the inside? Just imagine if your thoughts, mini-movies, and internal conversations that played through your mind, along with the feelings that you felt, were all projected out publicly on a news feed style forum. What would those who follow you see, and have access to? What would the world really think of the contents of your most personal possession, your private and personal inner world, your constant companion...**your mind**?

Mental health appears to have a stigma around it. It doesn't seem cool to have a mental disorder, or to struggle with the contents of your mind. I personally went through years of my life having repetitive negative and difficult thoughts, that left me feeling emotionally low and depressed. Having been through that difficult period, to now coaching others on how to change and improve their mindset, I personally know that it can seem as though you're weak to express that you're suffering within, and at times it can seem difficult for others to be patient, to understand, or to even step into your shoes to realise that you are in pain.

How do you express that you feel constantly on edge? Do you need to Instagram a picture of yourself leaning over the edge of a cliff, trying to hold on, trying to find a way to pull yourself together with the hashtag – #*this is what it feels like inside my mind and body*? Is this what it takes, nowadays, for people to stop rolling their eyes and telling you to 'pull yourself together', 'don't worry about it', or simply, 'relax you'll be fine'? Perhaps a YouTube vlog of you alone on a sinking ship, steadily going down, desperate to hold on, trying not to drown, whilst you keep the perfect hair, in the perfect outfit, holding on to the most current trending smartphone will send out a clear message of, *'this is what it feels like to be me'*. 'You'll be fine', they tell you. 'Don't let it bother you', they unemotionally utter. What does it take to get others to understand that getting out of bed and being you, living your life and having your mind, your thoughts, and the feelings that you feel, is difficult for you? Maybe it is a selfie that would make things better? Just smile on the outside as you crumble on the inside. Who needs mental health anyway? You can filter it out. You can pretend to keep it all together. No one else is showing his or her weaknesses. No one seems to be using the hashtag, *#cantcopewithmymind*

Perhaps the futuristic suggestion of instantly downloaded thoughts and exposure to all that occupies your mind would actually change the ways that individuals behaved towards one another? Imagine each thought that entered your mind, and each conversation that you had with yourself and also listened in on, projected out to those who follow you and know you. The behaviour of those around you would surely change, right? Would our hearts open up as we began to see the internal Britney Spears style breakdowns of 2007 happening on a daily basis, within the minds of those who we love and care for? Perhaps we would collectively and more consciously rise up to embrace one another with love and support, as we release the need to judge and compare our own personal wellness, as we collectively begin to care more for one and other? Is it really an app, a device, or another social media platform that we need to bring us together? Would that help us to see the pain and suffering on the inside, behind those filters, behind those hashtags, actually needs more mental care, love, and support?

There's no need for you to feel under pressure to have a perfect inner world; you may wonder if it's even possible. It's ok to feel emotionally low and it can take time to turn things around for the better, but it can be done.

It seems that for many people these days, the outer world and what is shared with others across their lives – even with those they don't personally know – is more important than the state of their inner worlds. With so much focus spent on projecting the image of having a perfect life, surely some time spent paying attention on your internal world, the screen that fills your mind, and also the sounds and conversations that play out within you would allow you to feel better within yourself?

Are there ways that you know of to help you cope with the content that fills the screen and space in your mind, or do you just ignore and brush off the contents that you view, listen in on, and spend time engaging with inside your own head? If I'd known back then what I know now, and what I'm going to show you, for how to change and improve your own thoughts and state of mind, then I would have found a sense of peace within, earlier in my life.

Your online world may seem perfect. It may be filled with unicorns, angels, and glitter, but let's consider the **news feed of your mind**. This is the real you, the only you. It is the you that only you know. No number of online likes will ever equal the amount of self-love and self-care only you can give to yourself. If you don't like yourself, what's the point in accumulating validation from people you barely know?

Knowing how to care for your own mind and your personal inner world with ways that help you to self-nourish, will bring you peace that benefits you right down to the depths of your soul. This level of satisfaction can be achieved, even if you feel challenged by the contents of your mind, you can learn several different techniques that will make you feel like you have more control, which will allow you to experience a variety of mental and emotional benefits in your life. The red hearts and blue thumbs of your online world will only scratch the surface of your mind. Why not work on a deeper level with the news feed of your mind so that you can bring more comfort and joy to your heart? Instead of yearning for more followers, why not experience how to be the leader of your own life and mind?

If you struggle with the contents of your mind and with the internal thoughts and conversations that you scroll through within, then knowing how to find relief is paramount to your mental and emotional health. Trust me, as you come to learn how to actively use your mind for a minimum of five minutes a day, you too can feel the same relief and ease I feel, and that my clients have also felt in their minds. There's a huge epidemic of social media posts that clearly show large quantities of individuals who are choosing to squat it out weekly to get the perfect Kardashian derriere. You may even try time after time to get 'lean in fifteen' with the hugely motivating Body Coach, but can you actually cope with your own personal thoughts?

Your honest and authentic world within doesn't have to be shared on a public scale, and it doesn't have to be perfect. Putting the *Black Mirror* style suggestion of accessing your mind to one side, the truth is that you alone experience your mind and your thoughts each and every day. I personally know that this can be a struggle; however, finding mental and emotional relief for whatever makes you anxious or for whatever drops you into the state of depression can be learned, programmed, and executed on a daily basis, leaving you with more mental and emotional ease.

 How would it feel for you to have more control, more ease and more relief mentally and emotionally?

Learning how to filter out your thoughts and mental movies can be as easy and effective as applying a Snap Chat filter. Difficult thoughts and memories can expire and disappear for you, just like an Instagram story. There's no need for you to be the only viewer watching your difficult and at times uncomfortable thoughts play over on repeat. Trust me - *I'll show you how to cope.*

Let me make one thing clear for you: Life doesn't have to be perfect. You don't need to fit a norm, a trend, or to be completely in alignment with the spiritual talkers or wellness warriors of the social media world. This is a suggestion that I invite you to personally now experience, a suggestion that it's OK to be where you are, doing what you're doing, thinking what you're thinking and feeling how you're feeling. Why? Because life is life. You will have the good days and the hard days. You'll experience moments where life makes you feel like you're living your best life, and times where you can't pick yourself up of the sofa. Life is like that. Through all that you do in life, all that you share and say, you are the occupant of your own thoughts in each and every moment.

Considering this fact, wouldn't it be helpful for the place that you spend so much time – with yourself and with your thoughts – to be a place you actually want to be in, a place that you enjoy being in, a place that you can cope with living in? – your mind.

My suggestion to you is to go on a journey within yourself to make your inner news feed more comfortable, more bearable, and more habitable. You can work through the anxiety and fear, through the worry and pain, through the love and excitement, so that you can have more control and feel more at ease. Why not step into your own personal space to tidy and declutter, to delete and erase all that no longer serves you? You don't have to continue thinking in ways that may keep you kidnapped mentally and emotionally, suffering at the hands of your own mind and your thoughts.

You don't have to try to make life seem perfect, but you can attempt to begin to understand that **the thoughts that you think and the conversations that you have within yourself are always contributing to your mental and emotional states.** The state that you find yourself in will always influence the way that you behave, as what you are choosing to think and in effect believe, will ultimately shape how you live your life. So why not learn how to cope with the daily noise and traffic that flows through your mind, in ways that are as easy as you filtering a photo? Why not experience the power that you have to delete what's being replayed over and over in your mind, as easy as it is to delete the fifty bad selfies you once took?

To know your own mind is to really know yourself. This is an opportunity for you to have more control over what you think and feel and how your thoughts are being formed so that you can improve the experiences that you have in your life. Instead of feeling as if life is happening to you, this is a work in progress opportunity to filter out, to change and to edit, things that are happening to you, that serve no positive purpose in your mind, and in your life. It's like having the ability to step into your mind instead of stepping to the side to watch your thoughts from the position of a powerless observer. It can help you shape and transform your life for the better.

Your mental health is your true health and it will always set the tone of your life. Instead of feeling like you're too scared to speak out or not confident enough to express how you're feeling within or to ask someone to throw you a rubber ring in order to stop you from drowning within, I'm throwing to you now – with a lot of love and a lot of hope – a life jacket in your size and preferred colour, to help you reach calmer and more pleasant waters, mentally and emotionally. Let's explore the beauty of your inner world. Come with me now and allow me to share what I know for sure, which are the resources you have within yourself that can transform the way that you structure your experiences in your mind, and ultimately help you change your life for the better.

Let the life you live be a life
that you can stand
living in,
- in your mind.

Allow the thoughts that you think
to be thoughts that are
comforting and loving,
- especially for yourself.

Be open to trying again and again to
access the
many different ways that you
can make things better
mentally and emotionally
- for yourself.

Detach from the feeling of being lost, as
you
come to find the natural self-control
that you can apply to
various areas of
your
life.

Encourage the space of your mind to be a
place that is healthy and homely
for your thoughts, as the space
in which those thoughts reside
is your eternal home
- in this life.

Question:
If you
were to
lose everything
and everyone
from your life,
if you were
to have no
home, no
communication,
no internet,
no devices,
no money,
and no resources,
if suddenly
everything
and
everyone
was
gone-

**what would you
be left with?**

My answer –

Your mind.

Part I

The News Feed Of Your Mind

Chapter 1

Your Personal Profile

When you realise just how you are forming
your experiences within, you have the
power to change the way in which your
mind is working.

What's On Your Mind?

The date was March 9th, 2018 and as I opened up the Facebook app on my phone, the first thing that I noticed more than usual was the status update question, **'What's on your mind?'**. I sat and contemplated for a while for what was actually on my mind. Having been heavily distracted from bouncing from each social media app, scrolling, watching, liking and stalking, I suddenly became less distracted by the screen in my hand, and more aware of the screen inside my mind. I became increasingly aware that I was in fact distracting myself from a serious bout of anxiety that no one around me could actually see, as on the surface all looked well; however, the feelings in my body left me feeling on the verge of running to the bathroom, from the churning that was in my gut. The more I actually focussed upon the Facebook question **'What's on your mind?'**, the more aware I became of how the anxiety was playing out on the screen within, which was filtering down a variety of uncomfortable feelings into my body.

'What's on your mind?' *asked Facebook* – In all honesty, a variety of thoughts that I was going to have a car crash and die on the motorway, I internally answered.

I hated driving on the motorway and the very next day I was driving for two hours and twenty minutes to visit my parents for the weekend. My usual choice was to go and see my family by train; however, the last few journeys had been bungled by severe delays and poor service, which kept on chipping away at my highly held value of 'making good use of my time'. With no more time to spare for the abuses of the rail services, I had made the choice to drive, and on the day before I was due to leave, I found a serious case of anxiety had crept upon me for the journey ahead that I faced. My mind was a collection of thoughts, which was made up of mini-movies and scenes that I was watching, and a lot of inner chatter, which collectively was contributing to my anxiety.

(The words underlined below highlight to you the way in which my anxiety was being formed).

'What's on your mind?' *asked Facebook* – My life is about to end from a car crash on the motorway, <u>I kept</u> <u>thinking</u>. I'll never see the people I love again, (as their faces <u>popped up</u> in my mind). There is so much I want to live for, I <u>think</u> with <u>worry to myself</u>. I <u>continually</u> <u>imagine thought</u> after <u>thought</u>, the <u>worst</u> possible <u>scenarios</u> of me having a car crash. My body <u>feels</u> so <u>tense,</u> like I've <u>frozen</u>, all from the <u>thoughts</u> and <u>mini-movies</u> that are going through <u>my mind</u>.

It continues as I really begin to ponder the question that Facebook is asking me.

'What's on your mind?'- 'Don't drive' a <u>voice</u> within <u>says</u> <u>repeatedly</u> in a <u>fast</u> and <u>panicked tone</u>. 'Take the train, save yourself' the <u>voice</u> <u>continues</u> as it <u>mixes</u> in with the <u>images</u> and <u>movies</u> of the deadly roads that await me tomorrow. I don't want to die <u>I feel</u>, but I <u>imagine</u> the <u>thoughts</u> and the <u>voice</u> <u>continues,</u> and as my husband says goodbye as he leaves for work, the <u>voice</u> <u>in my head</u> <u>says</u> 'you'll never see him again'. This <u>feeds</u> the <u>fear</u>, the <u>feelings</u> <u>cripple</u> my <u>body</u>, but again you'd have no idea how fast my <u>heart</u> was <u>beating</u>, how <u>short</u> my <u>breathing</u> was, and how <u>tense</u> I <u>felt</u> in my body from the <u>thoughts</u> and <u>conversations</u> that were going on <u>in my mind</u>.

This was the structure of my anxiety experience, which all happened at a great speed on the screen inside my mind. As I watched the action play out, and as I listened in on the frantic and fearful voices dominating the space inside my head, my anxiety continued to grow at a rapid speed.

 Are you aware of how your thoughts may be causing you to feel in a particular way from the way in which your mini-movies, scenes and internal sounds play out on the screen inside your head?

Opening the Facebook app made me realise the true reality of what was actually going through my mind. If I had updated my status update with the truth, with the content of my mind, I'm sure it may have raised alarms with my friends and family. Instead, I didn't share the truth of my inner turmoil; I pretended everything was perfect and chose to keep up with the Kardashians and everyone else who posts the 'perfect life', as I posed and pouted in an Instagram selfie with the hashtag #readyfortheweekend. The reality of the true state of my mind was far from ready for the weekend, and this was a true reflection of what I was going through as Facebook made me ponder the question; **'What's on your mind?'.**

🏠 How often do you really share **what's on your mind?**

🏠 How often are you aware of **what's happening inside your mind** that may be causing you to uncontrollably feel in a particular way?

The state of my mental health was in a difficult position, for out of nowhere, I had put myself in a situation where I had chosen to drive on the motorway that I had a fear of, instead of my usual choice of getting the train. This fear, I will add, was in fact quite mild; I'd rate its strength at 40%. This is because I've been aware of it in the past when I had previously driven, and like most anxieties, it disappeared, as the journey was smooth and not as stressful as I had anticipated. I had overcome this mild anxiety in the past by simply 'getting on with it' and making myself drive on the motorway, where each journey had been easy, and my anxiety had disappeared. The fear I had felt in the past only lasted briefly in the anticipation of the drive and it was previously quite weak in its strength. It didn't captivate or prevent me from travelling, as I managed to make my past journeys with ease, where the anxiety disappeared. What I observed this time however, was that my anxiety had come back stronger and with a vengeance. This showed me the state of my mind, which had now become more evident to me in the imminent time leading to my journey, from the overwhelming experience of anxiety that was now stronger than I'd ever experienced before.

Being an experienced NLP Master Practitioner and wellbeing coach with a repertoire of tools, I began to work on myself to dissolve and control the anxiety. It was also through my experience and knowledge as a practitioner that I was able to distinguish how my anxiety was being formed. I was able to take a step back to watch the crippling content play out frantically in my mind and having observed its developing strength, I got to work on myself to feel more at ease inside my mind. Again, no one would have had a clue that I was executing these helpful tools and techniques within. I was now working on the mini-movies and images – both moving and still – along with the internal dialogue that was freaking me out, to help ease the feelings that the actions of my mind were creating. I was dealing with what was on my mind and continued to do so as I went along my journey, which was easy, safe, and comfortable. I worked on 'setting' my responses to driving on the motorway with some positive mental and emotional NLP anchors. I knew that my state of mind needed some work for this issue, and because I was feeling comfortable on the motorway, I was able to work on myself to reassure the anxiety within that I was in fact, safe. Not only was I able to notice the way my anxiety was being formed and how it had increased in its strength, but I could apply my own tools and techniques to the state of my own mind. Success was mine, and the anxiety eased, but really my question to you, just like Facebook asks is, **'What's on your mind?'.**

The words that I've previously underlined will highlight to you the internal structure that was forming my anxiety. There was a **combination of thoughts** in the form of **images** and **mini mental movies**. There was **inner talk**, a **panicked voice** that **spoke fast with negative beliefs** that I was in danger, and also the **feelings** that I felt physically that were **caused** from the **thoughts and sounds that were happening inside my head**.

What's on your mind? Are you aware of the ways in which your mind is forming your experiences?

Each experience will differ in the structure and setup; however, there will tend to be similarities in the ways in which your thoughts and internal sounds build up your experiences inside your mind. In knowing **what's on your mind**, or rather <u>what's happening inside your mind,</u> and most importantly *how it's happening*, you place yourself in a position to change and edit the 'structure' so that you too can take control from the inside to change and improve how you think and feel within. There's no need for you to be so honest and open in updating your Facebook status with the true content of your personal inner world; however, in knowing that you can now learn to understand and most importantly change the pattern and structure of your own thoughts, you can now come to experience more mental and emotional ease for yourself.

The screen that sits in your hand as you scroll and swipe from each app, may be a lot easier for you to manage and switch off from than the screen that sits inside your mind. You can however, come to be in a position from what I offer to share with you, for the ways that you too can make the **'news feed' of your mind** a lot more comfortable to live with. It may be easy for you to filter out your reality online, and to post the highlights of your life when really, you're challenged in your mind. So, as you come to understand the many ways that you can now learn how to deal with **'What's on your mind',** your true reality can be one of more mental and emotional ease.

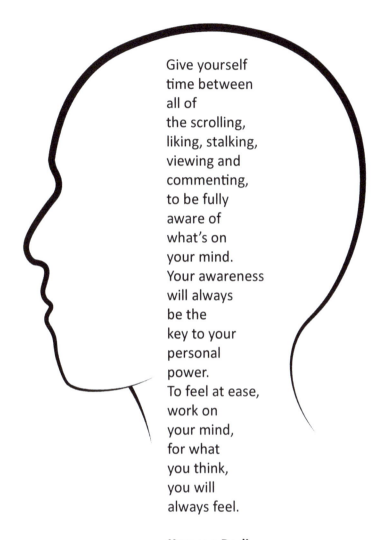

Give yourself
time between
all of
the scrolling,
liking, stalking,
viewing and
commenting,
to be fully
aware of
what's on
your mind.
Your awareness
will always
be the
key to your
personal
power.
To feel at ease,
work on
your mind,
for what
you think,
you will
always feel.

Kamran Bedi

Friends For Life

From as far back as I can recall, I can remember how I spent so much time in my mind planning for the future that I dreamed of. I used to spend so much time with my thoughts, contemplating all that could possibly be. Upon reflection, I can also remember the specific time in my teens when I spent months, if not years, anxious and fearful of going out and about because I had been mugged in my early years. Feelings of fear would cripple me, and upon reflection, **I can see the patterns of the troubled thoughts that fed those problematic feelings** I had for such a long period of my life. I can now see that back then, without knowing, I kept that fear running through the thoughts I chose to think. No matter if it was thoughts of worry, fear, happiness, or joy, thinking was something that I've always spent a lot of time doing. My mind has always been the place where I really spent most of my time, and as I drift so naturally in and out of my thoughts, I guess **I consider my mind as my permanent home.**

It's quite amazing how quickly you can get distracted and move forward or backward in time, all from the direction of your thoughts. It's all too easy to think and then feel the positive and negative contents of your mind. I'm sure that you also spend a lot of time binge-watching back-to-back episodes of a variety of different thoughts and mental movies inside your own head, just like I do. Whether it's the screen of your phone or the screen of your mind, there's always something that you're consuming.

In my recent years working as an NLP Master Practitioner and Trainer, I've also used Integral Eye Movement Therapy (IEMT), Mindfulness and Hypnosis in my work, to help me understand the patterns of thinking and the actions that so many individuals perform within their minds and with their thoughts. Thinking is natural and can take up so much time and energy, it can also dictate and control the type of life that you live. I found it quite alarming the number of years that people have suffered at the hands of their own thoughts, being unaware of how to use and improve their own state of mind. The longer that you struggle mentally, the heavier and harder it can feel to carry the weight of your world from your own thoughts. You may have experienced this yourself, however, this doesn't have to be the case. I've been inspired by seeing so many dramatic and instant changes that stemmed from the work that I do. In becoming aware of how your mind is working, it can really give you a deeper insight as well as more control into the power of your own thoughts. It's almost like you have this amazing built-in software system in your mind, which updates so regularly from the content of the world around you, yet you were sold short because someone, somewhere forget to give you the user's manual to your own mind.

How would life change and improve for you if you developed ways that helped you to reduce any stress or anxiety, so you could stop the feelings of overwhelm from an overactive mind?

As we continue to be mentally and emotionally overly stimulated with access to so much news and information, social media, apps, forums, endless selfies and opinions, we are continually switched on with our thoughts and emotions. This can lead us to our positive and negative feelings being over heightened. Our minds have to process and digest so much information that we consume. This can move almost like a rollercoaster, with the drops and dips that we feel and experience mentally and emotionally, each and every day.

Knowing the amount of information for your mind to consume and process, it has become clear to me that the state of one's mental health, for many individuals, always seems to be last on the list of their priorities. Bodies and diets tend to come first. People tend to spend time and finance on looking good, but not so much on learning how to cope with the tornado of thoughts and emotions rising within that can't be seen by others. Excuses and also limited knowledge or experience of how you can actually cope mentally, is also a definite issue when consulting with people over their mental health. For many, it's much easier to choose to be distracted, however, being distracted by consuming all that's around you, may detach you from what's consuming you from within, but only for a short amount of time.

Wherever you go, your mind goes with you. The thoughts that you think, the memories that bring, you pain, and joy are all transportable and accessible through the data files of your unconscious mind. You can re-live an experience, seeing it playing over and over in your mind, hearing the same sounds and feeling the feelings you felt then, if not stronger, all within the space of your thoughts. As you move from room to room, hallway to landing, inside or outside, from work to a bar, your mind and your thoughts, the inner conversations and your experiences go with you, each and every day. You may have forgotten so much of what once was, and there may be other content that just won't go away, taunting you like a toddler back and forth, loud and quiet, persistent in its need to be noticed. Smiling on the outside can seem all too easy, and so natural and normal; however, crying and crumbling on the inside may be your reality, as you fall helplessly into the content that consumes you from within.

Your mind is where all the action takes place. You may lie in bed at night filled with a montage of troubling thoughts that just won't let you sleep. Waking up in the morning may actually be more like waking up in your mind, as the thoughts that you think from the very start of your day are always there to meet you each morning as you watch, view, and listen to the content on your screen within. Right from the very start of your day you are thinking as you drift in and out of your mind. But as you take the role of being your own personal glam squad as you wash, dress, style, and contour, where are you in your mind?

🏠 What do you start your day thinking?

🏠 What are your morning thoughts for the day ahead?

🏠 Are your thoughts focussed on what happened yesterday?

🏠 Is your mind consumed with thoughts for pending problems?

In all of your day-to-day actions, as you walk and drive, cook and clean, and spend endless amounts of time scrolling on your phone, you naturally spend time in your mind; you're always in and out of your thoughts. You'll be forming ideas, images, and mental movies and also having internal dialogue and conversations inside your head, not only for content that you're experiencing on that day, but also for everything else that plays out from your past memories and also any future projections that play out in your mind. While you're sipping your coffee and buttering your toast, your mind is where you'll be existing. Think about the actions that you do and the full attention that you give to them and notice how much time you are spending in your private personal space of your thoughts. You can wave goodbye to your cat and step out of your physical home for your commute, when really, you're travelling through the thoughts in your mind. It's your thoughts that you drift in and out of, and the space within your head is that which you continually slip into and out of, all with great ease. Whether it's back to the past or ahead into the future, you naturally filter out the people and actions that are happening around you, as you step into the different layers, depths, and distractions of your thoughts.

At work, you could actually be mentally back at home, thinking about the argument you had with your spouse yesterday or the difficulties of your relationship. You may unconsciously work yet mentally ponder into your future – next week, next month, next year – as you effortlessly drift off into the world of your thoughts. You may be lying on the beach, and as you scroll on your phone, you can become mentally consumed by the actions of those that you do and do not know. This devours your time, taking you mentally and emotionally away from the paradise that you lie in. Your emotional mood and mental state can also be affected by the news and content that you read, and no matter how calm the tones of the beach and water that surround you may be, you can end up filtering out such beauty from the journeys you drift off to in your thoughts.

You can go anywhere in your mind, with ease and with no real reason; however, there is more comfort and relaxation in the freedom of the present moment, which can be sacrificed to an overactive mind. Your constant companion, your better half, your true best friend who's always been there for you, and who was with you for all that you've done and experienced, and will be there for all that happens in your life, is your mind. This is the true space where you live. It's where you spend so much of your time. **Your mind is your home.**

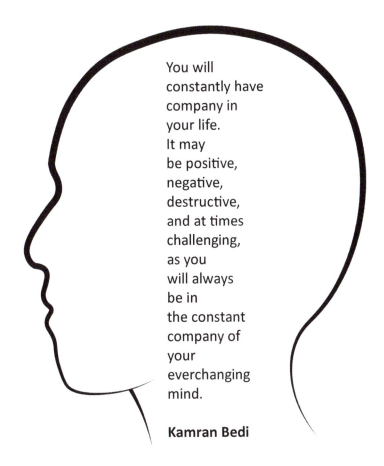

You will
constantly have
company in
your life.
It may
be positive,
negative,
destructive,
and at times
challenging,
as you
will always
be in
the constant
company of
your
everchanging
mind.

Kamran Bedi

Mindflix

You've definitely experienced that one person that you just couldn't get out of your head. I certainly have. There's the image of the person's face that popped up over and over as you showered, drove, ate and even when you were asleep, and it just wouldn't leave you alone. I used to get so frustrated when I just couldn't get the image of their face or the things they said out of my mind. It was also equally annoying the amount of time I spent binge-watching the annoyance that was caused, over on repeat on the screen in my head. How about you? I'm sure that you've analysed the things the person said, mixed and blended into scenarios and situations that you created in your mind, along with the pain they caused you, magnified from the thoughts that filled your screen within. There may have been the laughter and love that you had, or that you made up in your mind as you watched or imagined, thought after thought, filling the space of your mind. I've had those reoccurring, distracting, and consuming thoughts of love, and also pain, both positive and negative. It's all too easy to spend time binge-watching your thoughts on the screen inside your own head.

🏠 How much time did you spend thinking about that one person?

🏠 How many thoughts did you emotionally feel as you drifted into the world of your mind?

On the outside, life may have appeared happy, but on the inside, that one person was there in your mind, the apple of your eye, the cloud within your emotional storm, the one who helped form the reoccurring thoughts that just kept on coming. You've definitely replayed and re-analysed the internal dialogue, the conversations that got you mad, the things you should have said, and the things that you perhaps will say one day. You may still continue to play the inner chatter over and over, along with the scenes on the screen within as your mind entertains you or plagues you from the experiences that happened in the past but are still presently happening within your thoughts. It may have been weeks, months, or even years since an event occurred, yet it is at the forefront of your mind, physically out of sight, yet mentally with you everywhere you go.

🏠 How do you move past these thoughts?

🏠 Is it even possible to go beyond the thoughts that you think, and the internal conversations that you have?

🏠 Is it them or is it you?

🏠 Do you have control over your mind, or does your mind have control over you?

I've often caught myself deep in the depths of my own thoughts about situations and experiences that I can't control that powerfully rob me of the present moment. Travelling down a track of distracting and destructive thoughts is a habit that I used to part take in often. Having more understanding and control of my thoughts, allows me to subscribe to the more uplifting and positive thought channels of my mind, which allows me to live a life of comfort in the **home within my mind.**

Your experiences that at times, play over on repeat in the movie theatre of your mind, can feel like you're binge-watching episode after episode, the events of your own life. You can get sucked into the boxsets of your past, as you watch back-to-back episodes of the experiences that once were, replaying the past over and over, painfully on repeat. You may at times watch the same episode or same season of your past experiences. You can even spend time creating possible future experiences that have yet to happen, as you think them through in the *'Mindflix'* account of your mind. Escaping the screen within and the sounds that seem to ring out aloud may appear to be difficult for you. In all that you do, in all the places that you go, your mind and those episodes may at times just constantly be there, with it feeling difficult for you to fully turn off from all that's playing through your mind. One event can last forever in your mind. One person can dominate the stage you watch within, talking and parading their words and actions, emotionally kidnapping you from the freedom that you want to feel inside yourself. I know this particular pattern all too well, from future thoughts of fear, to past thoughts of pain. Binge-watching my life through thoughts is something I've certainly done. Perhaps you've spent years re-watching, and re-feeling the episodes of your life without actually re-subscribing to the *'Mindflix'* account of your life movies that you really don't want to view? It's what naturally happens in the state of your own mind. **You re-watch, re-listen, and re-experience the bad the ugly, and sometimes the good.**

In a world of perfect profiles, subscriptions, filters, and controls, the perfect life on your external screen is easy to create for others to view. Most profiles have the option to **'Edit Profile'** so you have the choice to make it all seem and sound perfect. But as you begin now to turn your focus to the account of your own mind, logging in for a personal systems update will give you the opportunity to filter out and edit the content of your own thoughts and experiences that isn't giving you any positive purpose in your life. Let me explain: The content that you have floating around within your own head, will generally be made up of thoughts that are made up of images and mental movies, inner sounds, chatter, and a variety of inner voices that all contribute to the internal and external experiences that you personally have, and also emotionally feel.

Let's start with some of the inner sounds that play within the walls of the home of your mind.

Are you aware of the very many ways that you talk to yourself? They'll be the times when you discuss things with yourself, like when a choice needs to be made. Then there's the talking yourself out of situations; the *'don't do it'*, *'don't say it'*, *'leave it'*, *'they won't like it'*, *'he doesn't love me'*, *'stop now'*, *'what's the point'* type of self-talk that goes on in your mind. You also have the *'what if'* conversations that can fill you with anxiety, as you *'what if'* every possible and potential threat, as you hang on to the edge of your seat. Really none of it's going to happen to you - but hang on, - *'What if'*? Perhaps you tend to have the *'I'm not good enough'* chat or *'I'm not worthy enough'* self-talk going through your mind? The playlist and episodes of self-talk topics can be endless. The self-chat and inner talk can blend and mix into a noise of tones and voices, montaged into the thoughts and images that play out in the theatre of your mind. Episode after episode, you can end up watching and listening in on a continuous travelling marathon of self-talk, which when negative, **can lead to mental and emotional self-harming.**

🏠 How aware are you of the content that you watch and sit through that comes from within?

🏠 Are you a leading character who is physically active in the movies, episodes and situations of your own mind in your personal inner world?

What affect is the content within your 'Mindflix' account having on your life?

I've already presented to you a number of questions to encourage you to reflect on the 'set-up' and structure of your own personal profile, for your own personal thought patterns. You can choose to answer the questions as you read along, make notes separately if you wish, or mentally reflect on your own personal world from what I am presenting to you.

Following the internal sounds that I previously explained to you, you also have the gallery of thoughts formed in **stilled images** and **playing mental movies** that can fill your screen within or pop up out of nowhere.

Thoughts of your past can seem overpowering, as can mental movies of the future as you imagine and anxiously worry for what could happen, so personally and privately all in the space within your own head. Watching your life play out inside your head, for regrets of the past or concerns of the future may actually consume more time than you spend scrolling on your smartphone. Moving from your external screens to your internal screen can leave you feeling the emotional impacts of the material that you so freely watch and consume. Your mind can feel like a montage of content that's personal and private to you, which takes you on a physical emotional rollercoaster that at times can feel as though you've lost control of feeling the way that you want to feel or thinking the way that you want to think. Even though it's your mind and your screen within, escaping the repetitive screen play that can hijack and overpower your emotions, may feel impossible from the experiences that you've had in your own mind.

🏠 Do you have a mind filled with worry?

🏠 Does your internal screen play the events of your past over and over?

🏠 Is your body a container of uncomfortable emotion?

Questions, questions, and more questions that may lead you to ponder and reflect on the ways in which your internal world is 'setup' and 'running', to now gain a glimpse or various insights of how life is happening to you or for you, which all happens in your mind. This could be viewed and analysed in a variety of ways, but one observation that I'd like to draw your attention to, is in relation to the company that you keep, the place that you spend so much time, emotion and energy, the place where I think you permanently live, view, and listen in on, - **your mind.**

Whether you're scrolling or swiping your way through every app and profile you filter your life through, you are always conversing, thinking, and living, in the space of your own thoughts. Your thoughts are like the food that you choose to taste, chew, and digest. Each experience you have is mentally processed through your internal makeup of sounds and sights, filtered out by what you choose to see and hear, which you then swallow and digest into the gut of how you feel within. The content that rattles around inside your head, and the time that you spend re-watching and re-experiencing can be likened to you eating the same meal three times a day for the rest of your life. **When are you going to change the recipe that you're mixing together and the method that you're using that gives you the same experience from the thoughts and sounds that you mix inside the bowl of your own head?** You may be unaware, but that which you choose to focus upon, can be edited out and filtered out as easily as you change the content of your online profiles. You just need to be aware of a new method for the recipe of the mixture of your mind, so that you can think and feel better, (as you learn from me), to have more mental and emotional self-awareness and self-control.

You see, you are not any of the profiles that you share on social media. The number of followers you have, or the likes that you can muster up does not define you. You are not really the person that you want others to believe who you are. You are not limited; you are limitless; you are nothing and you are everything, as you are always going to be, feel, and experience the results of the contents of your own mind. No app can step into your actual world. No person can define the life that you live. Each day, each moment, each experience to have or to lose out on, is always – in effect – a choice of your own thoughts. To do, or not to do? To think and to then feel, each moment is merely a fragment of your mind. How long that fragment – that experience – lives on for, and how long the feelings that you feel are prolonged, all comes down to your choice. You can choose to play out and to re-live the content within, or to end the particular scene, as you move on to the next episode of your life in your mind through your thoughts.

Your yesterday may be the episode that seems so present in your mind. Perhaps you're still playing out something that happened five years ago when *'he said this'* or *'she did that'* as you feel the anger and emotion from the experiences that once were. Perhaps the future is more dominant in your world within, as you plan and create, hope and dream, or feel full of dread and worry created by the thoughts of your mind. Or are you actually present and feeling mentally and emotionally free where you currently are within your thoughts each and every day?

Your thoughts and the contents of your mind have the power to transport you back and forth, from love to pain, from mental highs to emotional lows, through each moment of each day. I have certainly experienced this myself, time after time. I was mentally and emotionally consumed by the experiences of my life that I entertained and allowed to overpower me, all in the home of my mind. You can come to understand and take any of the viewpoints that you are either one with your mind or you are, in fact, one accompanying your mind.

 Are you directing and leading, or watching and being led?

Whether you're with or alongside, aligned or being led, you are aware that there is more of you than that which meets the eye. More shades and more tones, some light and some dark, all of which resides within your personal and private head space. As you come to reflect upon and understand the position that you have with your mind, you may begin to see the different angles that you switch between during times when you view and times where you lead your mind through your experiences within. Perhaps you have a sense of the ever-changing personality that changes in context, experience, and the company that you are in, as you begin to see the types of persona, shape, figure, and strength of the ever-changing mind that lives inside your head?

 How can something that belongs to you, and that lives within you, change so easily in how it appears, thinks and makes you feel?

Do not panic about what you discover and see within your mind. Do not worry if the voice inside your head goes into hiding. In learning and reflecting of the patterns that form your experiences and shape your world inside and out, you can be led and guided to find peace or strength, to heal or to detach from the mind that you live in and out of. This whole observation and reflection that I deliver to you to ponder can, in itself, be analysed as quite an anxious pattern of reflecting and questioning, unsettled and searching through possibility after possibility. Really, how much more can you examine and wonder about the ways in which you are and the ways that you think?

I feel the facts are there. You think, you watch, you talk, and then you feel things over and over again inside your own head. Confusion can come all too easily. Worry can be ignited in a single thought, yet your options to change and transform your inner world with ease, can seem redundant. This is not the case.

I know all too well the ways that the mind works and the structures that create your experiences. I also know from observing daily actions that you so unconsciously take as you 'swipe' and 'scroll', 'like' and 'block', that you have the power within yourself to renovate the space within you where you experience your life mentally and emotionally. This power is widely accessible, and each action that you so effortlessly take can and will strengthen the focus you are now directing into the theatre of your thoughts.

To be in a position for your life to change, to edit, re-set and to update, you must be open to logging in to the personal profile to see and note who and how you are. Fear not for what lies within, for the skills that you are unaware of possessing are what we are now going to work with to shape and improve your mind from the inside out.

During every waking moment of every day you are in and out of your own thoughts walking, talking, and travelling the journeys within your own mind. At times, you may feel like a passenger, or you may feel as though you've lost control; however, it's your mind, your world, your vehicle that you move in, it's the place that you permanently live in, as **your mind is your home.**

🏠 How many more episodes of the past are you going to re-play in the movie theatre of your mind?

🏠 Are you ready to move your life forward to a new chapter or a new season that is current and enjoyable for you?

🏠 Do you need to unsubscribe from the *'Mindflix'* account that focusses on negative or problematic viewing?

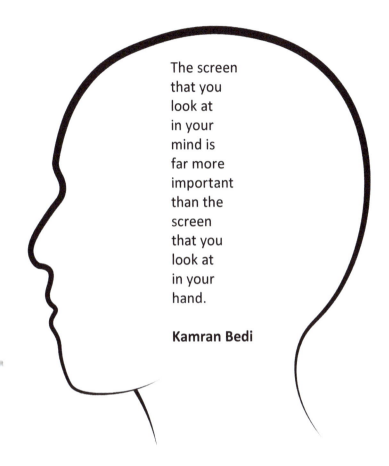

The screen
that you
look at
in your
mind is
far more
important
than the
screen
that you
look at
in your
hand.

Kamran Bedi

Chapter 2

LOGIN

People and experiences will come and go, but memories thoughts and feelings can be played over and over, and in practice they can last forever in your mind.

Headspace

Allow yourself to come to a position where you have more control and influence over the companion that you spend so much personal time with – your mind, and also the thoughts that your mind hangs out with. In your exploration of scrolling through **the news feed of your thoughts** and also the sounds that fill the space and screen within, let's look at how your thoughts are working, and whether they're working for or against you. In doing so, let's consider how your mind can travel so easily through space and time, off into the future and so far back into the past. Some of those 'time hops' may be quite pleasant, and others may fill you with emotional discomfort. Wouldn't it be easier to just swipe away those past painful reminders, as easy as you do on the screen of your phone?

You can probably think back to your earliest memory, and you may try harder to go further than the one stand out memory that keeps popping out for you. Travelling back and forth in your mind with your thoughts can seem so natural, and can take up a lot of your time and energy. Wherever you are, and with whatever you're doing, you can very quickly take yourself away from the present moment, without anyone even knowing what you're doing or thinking. Your ability to imagine back into the past or into the prospects of the future may have been a gold medal strength that you've always had.

🏠 Can you recall the times in your younger life where you dreamed of love?

🏠 Do you remember imagining the life that you would live, the places that you'd go to and the experiences that you'd hope for?

Back then, life may have been just a dream – a strong hope that someday you would get to do all that passed through your mind, thinking, hoping, and dreaming of what life would be for you. 'Please pay attention', your teacher may have asked. 'Concentrate more', your parents may have suggested. But still, the space in your mind was yours to adventure and to imagine all of the possibilities of your universe.

In your current adult self, your ability to wander into a world of thought may be as strong as it was for your younger self. Although now and in the current head space that you enter into, your thoughts may be something of a different catalogue that you flick through. Instead of dreaming of parental freedom to travel and to explore, your thoughts may be directed more to the anxiety and worry channels, as the only adventure you explore in your mind may always be connected to the reoccurring inner talk of *'well what if this happens?'*, and *'what if that happens?'*, dampening your ability to dream. Whether it's thoughts of love or thoughts of fear, you can very easily travel forwards and backwards in the time capsule of your mind. Time spent in your mind thinking and dreaming, to suggest and to explore may be something that you've always done with ease, and it's something that you will probably always be able to do.

Are you aware of the time that you spend with your thoughts, and more importantly are you aware of where you travel to so freely in your mind? Wherever you journey off to in your own personal head space, may or may not serve you well. You may be re-living the pain of yesterday feeling unable to switch your mind off. You may also venture off into the future feeling limited in your ability to stop yourself binge-watching the potential threats of your future that fill you with anxiety. Who actually knows how much time you spend in your mind with your thoughts, thinking through the situations in your life that have happened to you, as well as to the prospects of what could happen for you? How often have you spent time overthinking the worse-case scenarios and then none of it ever happens, yet you felt the anxiety and fear from your thoughts, which simply disturbed the potential ease and peace that you could have so easily have experienced instead?

You reportedly have anywhere between 12,000 to 60,000 thoughts per day, which is a lot of time to be spent thinking through your fears, especially if that's the direction which your thoughts head in. A lot of your thoughts tend to be repetitive in terms of the content that flows through the screen of your mind. The Groundhog Day of love can be exciting, yet the repetitive cycle of fear can feel exhausting and dictate how you live your life. Thought after thought, your mind is the one space and place that you've spent the most time in and will spend even more time with, through your entire life. You see, you're always thinking, even when you're doing. You can very easily drift off somewhere else for the slightest few seconds to ponder, to see, to discuss, and then feel, all from the actions of your mind. In conversation, you may be completely physically there, but mentally, you can escape and come back just in time to not be called out for not paying attention. It's the same when you're driving. You can set off on a journey, where physically you're driving to your set destination, but mentally you're on an entirely different journey as you travel with your thoughts. Your options of multitasking through your thoughts and actions are endless. You can probably scroll on your phone with your laptop on your lap, while going back and forth to Instagram on your phone, Facebook on your laptop, with the TV on in the background. Getting distracted by your thoughts as you go anywhere else in your mind when you're physically on the beach, distracted mentally when on a date, is something that you've always done, and something that you always will continue to do, probably with great ease.

This is how your world has come to be shaped and for how you're living your life right now. Whether you're fully aware or not, you will always think your way through each situation, each task and each moment, with your thoughts at times moving at the speed of light. Some thoughts you give very little time to, as the situations and circumstances automatically please your inner 'safety boxes', leaving them all ticked with little effort and great speed. Then there are those other situations that you still may play over, some from five years ago, re-living and re-feeling the pain and frustration, the anger and the tears, all in the space of your mind.

With every situation, your mind will naturally scan through and filter out anything unnecessary and highlight to you all of the necessary bits, until you feel a sense of control, safety, and inner peace. Even in your physical activities, and interactions with those around you, your internal search for safety and comfort will happen so quickly enough to allow you to feel safe in your own mind. If you don't fulfil the criteria that you've set, you'll express and react in potentially anxious ways – questioning, searching, and demanding answers in order to find your safety. The extreme of not knowing and not being able to naturally hit that inner self-comfort button, can lead to you sharing your panic and expression emotionally, physically, or even in a verbal anxiety or panic attack. Your mind is always working, it is always switched on and spending time in thought is what you've always naturally done.

As your mind is the space in which you spend most of your time, it will only come to positively serve you in ways that allow you to feel a sense of mind control with the 'set up' of your thoughts. As you commute from space to space and take part in each daily activity, you will always at times be in and out of the occupancy of your own mind. Whether your thoughts have been harmful or productive to you, or whether you feel you have the power to change and improve things within you, your mind is where you will mostly live. Your head space is your permanent, portable and private home. In understanding now that the mind that you have is the mind that you can develop and improve as a resourceful tool for you, your life can begin to improve beyond your fondest dreams.

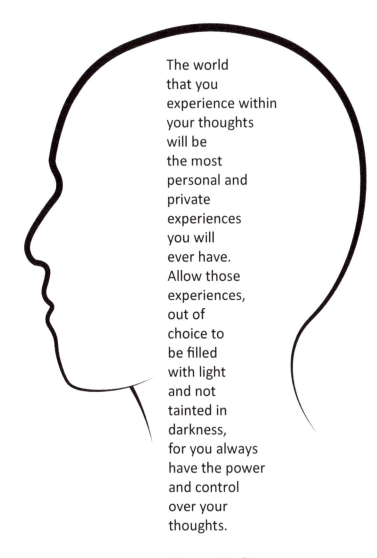

The world
that you
experience within
your thoughts
will be
the most
personal and
private
experiences
you will
ever have.
Allow those
experiences,
out of
choice to
be filled
with light
and not
tainted in
darkness,
for you always
have the power
and control
over your
thoughts.

Kamran Bedi

Edit Your Profile

From my insights into the ways of the mind for how thoughts, mental movies, inner talk, and conversations can dominate your internal news feed, which you continually scroll through within, you'll get more clarity on your own internal settings as we **step into the home of your mind.**

Deeper insights always come through self-searching, and there's no better way to get clarity than to ask some powerful questions that take your focus within. Take your time, think, observe, and step into the home that you have inside your mind. Allow yourself not to be distracted, to have this time for you, to make notes and observations, not to judge for what you find, see, and hear. I will then help you edit and transform the system of your mind, as we get to a complete renovation, later in this book. If you want, you can choose just to read and reflect now then answer the questions in detail later on.

Let's consider:

 Does your mind feel like it's with you or a separate part of you?

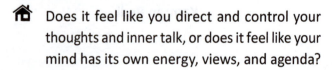 Does it feel like you direct and control your thoughts and inner talk, or does it feel like your mind has its own energy, views, and agenda?

🏠 Does your mind feel like it represents you or the views of others? If so, can you identify who is in your mind?

🏠 Does it feel light or dark within?

🏠 Is it cluttered? Loud? Noisy?

🏠 Does it feel tidy, peaceful, and comfortable?

🏠 If you could put a year or time period on the space inside your head, where are you?

🏠 Are you in a time of the past, the present moment, or off into the future?

🏠 What dominates you more within; thoughts, images, and mental movies or inner chatter, people's voices, perhaps negative inner sounds and talk?

🏠 Do you often think back to the good times you've had?

🏠 Do you have a positive inner voice within that reflects on the good in your life?

🏠 Do you often tell yourself that you're of great value to this world?

However your answers, your reflections, and your insights come across for you, do not worry if there is work to do within your mind. Do not fear if there is a lot to tidy and restructure. Do not panic if you don't like what you feel, hear, or see.

If you feel comfortable in the space within your mind, feel open to now learning how to maintain or even strengthen the space that you enjoy there. Wherever you personally are, the methods that I am going to cover with you can always potentially serve you well, mentally, and emotionally for any personal situation.

It can take great courage to look within, to be honest and open with yourself, and to look at what's working for you or against you. It can also be difficult and emotional; however, there are ways that you can cope, and ways that I will show you that will help you to think and feel better within.

Your mind, at times, can seem so heavy and hard to handle with the weight of your thoughts bearing down on your physical emotions, as the content of your mind repeats itself over and over, again and again. How many times have you mentally and emotionally suffered thinking the worst, fearing what would come, feeling angry for what you wanted to say – and then none of it ever happened? Yet you think, you feel, you ride a tsunami of different emotions, all experienced within the world under your skin. This can happen for hours, days, months, and even years as you spend time thinking and feeling the projections of your thoughts. You can think yourself back into fear and forward into worry. It's all too easy for you to feel the impact of your emotions from the journeys that you go on with your thoughts.

It's quite amazing what you can do with your mind. You can recall happy, loving memories; you can experience instant joy from exploring the past memories of your life, and you can feel motivated as you create the visions and dreams of your desired future. Your thoughts, your memories, your imagination of what you could create, can at times be so uplifting and pleasant, allowing your physical body to wash positively in the emotions your thoughts so effortlessly create. Perhaps this is something that you are aware of, or a way of thinking that you engage with?

The flip side that you may know all too well, though, is how quickly you can get stuck in a cycle of negative thinking. Fear can dominate you, and your thoughts can leave you feeling paralysed with anxiety from the sounds, images and movies that play out within. The inner voice of panic can scream loud and true, encouraging you to avoid living your life as you end up being held captive to the negative narrative that controls all that you do. This is what you do in your mind. This is what others do with their thoughts. **This is what those around you may grow up to experience and become experts in 'doing'.** Wouldn't it be wonderful for you to be in a position to improve your own mental health and to then share what you know with those younger minds in your life? Your ability to improve how you feel spreads further into educating those around you so that they too can take control and they can also learn how to cope within.

Through the realisation of looking into your mindset, the patterns and strategies that are in place that may lead you to thrive in life, as well as those in areas that may at times cause you to hide away in life, you can begin to understand the structure of your own mind. In learning not only how your mind is functioning, but more importantly in understanding the ways that you can find instant relief from the experiences of the past, and also find peace over worrying for your future, you can very quickly come to a position where you can transform your life. **This is what I am going to show you.**

The mind that you live in and the environment that is created within from your thoughts and your experiences will always be personal to you. You could be having the most relaxing massage, yet mentally still re-living the work meeting that didn't go well for you days before. Wouldn't life be better for you to be there, where you are? Less occupied, less emotionally on edge? Don't worry I'll demonstrate how you can have more control of your thoughts.

Your life is always going to be how you choose to experience each day, and how you process each experience on the inside with your thoughts. You can re-live the pain and anger of yesterday or even last year, and you can be fearful of what is yet to come in your future. You can also use the same mind to improve how you're thinking to experience closure for what once was, as you think of peace for what could possibly one day be. **It all starts and ends with your thoughts.**

You can be rich with financial security, yet poor in how you operate your mind. You can have the latest trending gadgets, but be unable to think in new and empowering ways. You can seem happy on the outside, yet you may be suffering on the inside. You may think your life is hard, but to others, it may seem easy. Rich or poor, young or old, black or white, gay or straight, trans, man or woman, you live in the occupancy of your mind. What you experience as pain within, another is suffering in their own way. What keeps you up at night is the same pattern of thinking that causes others to also lose sleep. Your mind is no different in its ability to go from love to pain, joy to fear, peace to stress, or worry after worry. It's what we all do so well. We are a nation of thinkers, living our lives from the inside with our perceptions of the outer world being reflected mentally and emotionally on our own internal screens. No matter how wide you smile, or how loud you cry, almost everyone you know experiences their internal worlds – both happy and sad – in a way that's similar to you. When you know and most importantly experience, how you can change and transform the patterns of your mind to improve and enjoy the experiences of your inner world, you can begin to feel the limitless, unrestricted power of your mind. This is a hugely important position to be in, as it is with your mind that you will always be united with and eternally in the company of as you journey on through this life.

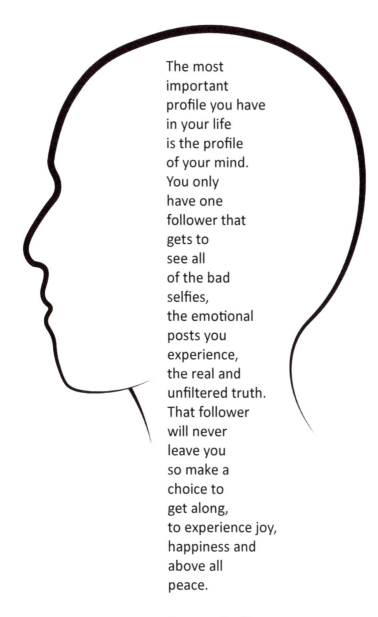

The most
important
profile you have
in your life
is the profile
of your mind.
You only
have one
follower that
gets to
see all
of the bad
selfies,
the emotional
posts you
experience,
the real and
unfiltered truth.
That follower
will never
leave you
so make a
choice to
get along,
to experience joy,
happiness and
above all
peace.

Kamran Bedi

Your Mind Is Not The Enemy

No matter what you've personally experienced in your life, allow yourself to come to a position of endless possibilities now, as you choose to open and expand your mind to changing and transforming the thinking patterns that may not be serving you any positive purpose in your life. As you begin to reflect on your own state of mind – and before we get into changing and improving your own personal set up – remember that your observations may have led you to see that your mind is, in itself; **its own entity.** Let's consider the following to help you get some deeper insights into the structure and system of your own mind, before we go on to learning how to deal with the content that lives within.

🏠 As you feel yourself going from place to place, living your life and taking each day as it comes for you, is your mind with you, or does it feel as though you have a travelling companion that goes wherever you go?

🏠 Does your mind feel like a guest that's perhaps overstayed its welcome?

🏠 Have you got a tenant living within that needs to be evicted?

🏠 Does your mind resemble a tantrum taunting loud child who won't leave you alone? Or is there another character type that fits the energy that speaks, moves and lives within?

🏠 Has your mind been playing the same difficult stories and memories over on repeat?

🏠 Does your mind express fear and anxiety for the future?

Let's look for further insights into your personal head space. Just imagine the contents of your mind as the rooms within your personal home.

🏠 What would you be stepping into each and every day as you look into the environment of your mind?

🏠 How would the environment of your physical home feel if it displayed the environment of your mind?

🏠 What would be written on the walls, watched on the TV, and played through the speakers from the thoughts, mental movies, and conversations that you have within your own mind?

Any environment is always going to influence how you feel personally within yourself. In reflecting upon the environment of the home of your mind, you can begin to look at what needs changing and improving as you now come to a position to re-decorate and renovate the structure of your mind.

🏠 Is there too much clutter within?

🏠 What's out dated that could go into the trash?

🏠 Does your mind feel light and bright or heavy and dark?

In the space of your mind, you will at times talk to yourself as you drift from past conversations, talking them through your mind, to times where you are not conversing but instead only listening to one of the many inner voices within yourself that are talking to you or at you. You may also at times replay past conversations or voices of others, repeating and re-listening to the words and conversations that you can't seem to move away from. You may have so many different voices passing through your mind changing for different situations and circumstances that it can, at times, contribute to anxiety, worry, and crippling fear.

🏠 Have you ever noticed that the voice within sometimes isn't your own voice?

🏠 Have you begun to identify that some voices are stronger and some are weaker?

It's not just a playlist of different conversations that fills the space of your mind. You, yourself, will also have thoughts that sit prominently in your mind, for present situations, past experiences, and even potential future situations that you imagine. You can spend a lot of time and energy thinking out so many thoughts and repeatedly playing out mental movies of real situations and possible scenarios, which all influence your personal mental and emotional state.

🏠 Begin to notice or even look back at how easy it has been for you to drift away from where you are and what you're doing, to somewhere and something completely different in the space of your mind.

🏠 Can you notice the genre of thoughts that you often visit, or wonder off into?

🏠 Are you aware of the emotional states you personally put yourself into from the mental movies, inner talk, and the stories of the past and the concerns of the future that take over your personal and present state?

🏠 Are you walking in the park? Driving through the countryside? Lying on the beach? At diner with those you love? **Or are you scrolling and swiping through the news feed of your mind?**

As you begin to become aware of the ways in which your thought patterns and thinking strategies are forming your experiences, you'll realise you can make changes in your life. How? **It begins with your awareness**. Even as you notice whether the actions that you choose are consciously or unconsciously influencing you to become distracted from the ease and joy of each present moment, you can begin to understand that you have a variety of choices to help you improve and change your experiences within. These choices will follow shortly. In understanding the ways in which your mind is 'working' and the various ways that your content is presented and represented on your screen within, **your awareness is the first step in you taking your own personal power**. You have the choice to learn how to use your mind more productively, and the choice about how to take action to be more mindful and more present. But most powerfully and most importantly, you have the choice to change and to improve, to influence and enhance, to renovate and to modernise the home of your own mind.

Through the majority of the work that I've done with individuals as a coach, one of the clear patterns that I've seen time and time again is how so many people feel they are in some ways a prisoner to their own minds. Whatever the experiences may be that they are challenged with, to them it feels as though there are constant reminders of their past problems or current challenges being replayed over and over, watched, heard, and felt that causes them personal discomfort. This can all contribute to elements of depression, stress, anxiety, fear, lack of confidence, and general mental and emotional turmoil. These individuals have sat across from me, describing all that is happening to them in their minds and in their lives, as if they are spectators who have a front row seat to the film that they just don't want to watch anymore. For some, this difficulty has played out for over twenty years, causing a lifetime of mental and emotional strain. The common problem that so many feel is that they are at the mercy of their own minds, unable to cope, and unaware of ways in which they can find mental and emotional relief.

Imagine waking up each day to watch the same problematic scene on your television before you started the day. Imagine the Groundhog Day-like routine of repeating the same painful memories of yesterday, when all you want to do is to turn the screen off and not be forced to watch the torment of what was. Perhaps listening to the same difficult and painful conversations about what once was or for what could potentially be playing through your mind is something you could also imagine or even relate to? Is this the type of playlist that runs through your head? Fear, worry? Anxiety about what's to come? Anger, regret, or guilt for what has happened in the past?

In whatever way you choose to look at the place that you live in inside your head, you will generally find that at times you feel comfortable or uncomfortable, all in the space of your own mind. The internal structure of how your thoughts are formed will change for each individual experience and there will be times where your mind is your best friend and times where your mind will feel like your worst enemy. Some things will feel easy for you to get over, and others will play over and over, taunting you like there's no tomorrow. Some inner conversations will fill you with dread, and others will warm your heart. Life will always be a continual change and flow of energy as you move from day to day, each moment reflecting, processing, and experiencing all that happens to you. In realising that your mind may be stuck in how it's performing, or perhaps assessing the types of tones and conversations your inner voice has been having, you can now come to be in a position to understand that **your mind is not the enemy.**

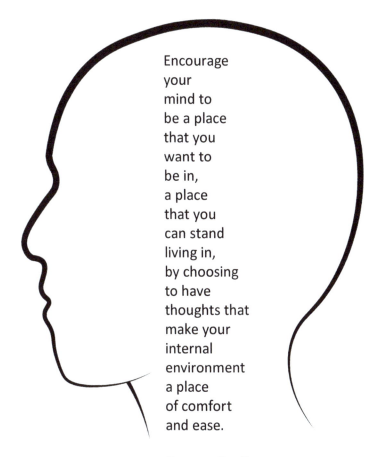

Encourage
your
mind to
be a place
that you
want to
be in,
a place
that you
can stand
living in,
by choosing
to have
thoughts that
make your
internal
environment
a place
of comfort
and ease.

Kamran Bedi

What I Know For Sure

For many years, I was in so many ways, a prisoner of my own mind. The thoughts that I would think held me captive to the fear that paralysed me mentally and emotionally. **On the surface, I seemed as though I had it together.** Although I thought that I depicted a character to those around me that was happy and in control, **on the inside, I was taunted, tortured and teased by the thoughts that lived in my head,** which occupied the screen of my mind. The slide show of scenarios was full of fear. The uncertainty over my life left me confused in so many ways that my mind played over and over the fearful possibilities that wrenched my gut emotionally. I was, for so long a victim to my own mind. I felt powerless, unable to change or escape the channel of thoughts that kept on showing up, brighter and stronger, making me feel so uneasy in my own skin. Smile and dance. Talk and nod. On the outside I was there, but on the inside a cyclone of thoughts plagued my mind and emotions, which was destroying me slowly, as the pain of my mind grew stronger. There was no ceasefire, there was no inner peace. With the same speed as flicking a switch, fear would fill me, and my mind would play over the dark thoughts, as I lived with the fear that rattled within me.

I know from my own experience the mind's ability to catapult you deep into the darkness of your thoughts, and how easy it is to get stuck there. It's easy to become a victim on the inside, as the inner voice screams in pain, from the thoughts that fill your mind. It is difficult to escape or to find relief from those torturous thoughts. I know how the mind can strengthen in its power to think of every possible fearful situation, which leaves your inner world shaking with worry, as you struggle to escape being in the company of yourself. Thoughts can over power you, and inner talk can prevent you from living your life as you become directed by the manifesto that is spoken within your own head. Inner chaos can seem too familiar; and I know that the ability to speak up, to seek help or to share your pain can seem inaccessible, even if the words to describe your turmoil can seem incomprehensible for you to put together. I know that you think that others won't understand you, or that they'll brush off seeing your turmoil as unimportant. I know you can feel stuck and limited by the mind that is yours, that in turn has become your biggest and most personal annoyance. From experience, I also know that wherever you go, your thoughts go with you. Even in the happiest times you can be fully present in the company that you are in, laughing, talking, and bonding with those who you love, yet in the back of your mind, your thoughts are lurking, pacing through the hallways within your head, reminding you that they are not going away. I know that escaping your thoughts is all too easy.

Distractions are available everywhere. You can scroll and swipe, smoke and drink, laugh and cry – just do not think. The beast within may rest at times, but it's dominance will always return to capture you.

I know that it's all too easy to live in the pain of your mind, and that it's difficult to find ways to detach, to stop, and to deal with those reoccurring thoughts. I know that however hard you try, those thoughts keep coming back and over time they seem stronger and more forceful, influencing your mood, your interactions and how you see the world around you. You can end up feeling defeated, emotionally low as you feel powerless for any prospect of peace that you simply long for: peace within your mind.

I know from experience that your thoughts can make you ill. Your physical body can speak the pain of your mind, through your skin, and through your health, for your body will always physically and emotionally express the contents of your mind. I know that your mental health should be encouraged to be taken more seriously, like you wouldn't leave a physical cut to bleed for years without paying attention to it, hoping that one day it would just disappear. I know that working on your physical health is always encouraged; however, I also know that a healthy heart aligns well with a healthy mind.

I know through my own experience, having moved from pain and into peace. From not knowing to being certain and in control. From being lost, to finding my way. From being trapped to feeling free. From the unknown to discovering wisdom. From hurting, to healing. From being limited to being limitless, that your mind is the greatest asset that you possess, and that the thoughts that you choose to think will either be constructive or destructive for your own mental and emotional health. I know that within you, you have the power to change and transform any situation that you face in your life, in any moment and in any time, by simply choosing to engage your mind, and by changing the thoughts that are creating your experiences within. Your limitless and powerful mind has the ability through the direction that you instigate, to change the direction that your life is going in, simply through one single thought.

I know that the same way in which fear can be created is the same way that hope can be found. The same way that worry can consume you is the same way that joy can lift you out of the darkness of your mind. I know that you may feel that your thoughts have mentally brought you to your knees, and I know that you can and will rise to stand again. For what I know for sure from having been there, to now being here, is that you have more power than you think you know you have.

I know that everything always starts in your mind, with your thoughts, from the way in which you react to a situation, to the way that you understand a situation.

You were born and educated in ways that helped you to receive and interpret information, in which you now have the ability to process and experience life quicker than you can blink your eye. Your ever growing and expanding mind can take in information faster than you can say your name. In those interpretations that fit within the map of your world and how you understand the world around you, you are always reacting to and understanding your experiences from what you believe to be true. This leads to how you communicate, the language that you use, the tone that you express which always feeds the emotional body that you so instantly feel and experience within yourself. Your thoughts that dictate the way you see an object are not limited to what you think you know, for I know that your mind can expand and discover new ways of thinking and living, from this very day.

You may feel powerless to change and improve the movie in your mind and the inner commentary that has played over on repeat, and also the pain and suffering that your mind has led you to believe, that in some cases, has defined who you are. However, I do know that you are not stuck in a particular space, you are simply stuck in your mind. You are not lost on your life journey, you are lost in your mind.

I know that it's the same mind that causes problems, that is the same mind that can produce solutions. The same mind that causes pain, is same mind that can allow you to experience joy. The same mind that allows you to feel aroused, is the same mind that can heal your body. The same mind that you were born with, is the same mind that you are currently living in. Life may at times have been easier for you in your past, it may have felt less problematic at times, yet it is the same mind that you had then that you also possess now.

For **what I know for sure** is that you may at times feel that you need rescuing from your own thoughts; however, it is the mind that you feel is seeking help, which is the same mind that can rescue and save you now.

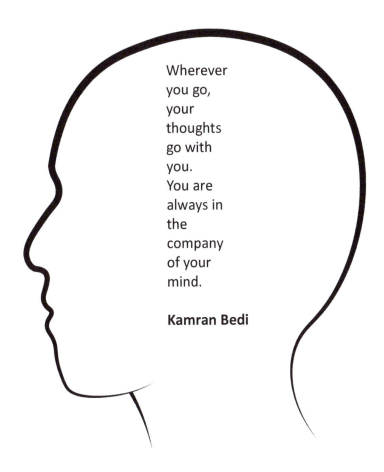

Wherever
you go,
your
thoughts
go with
you.
You are
always in
the
company
of your
mind.

Kamran Bedi

Part II

Mind Refurbishment

Chapter 3

Working From The Inside Out

The world that you experience within can now be a place that's full of resources to allow you to simply thrive in your life.

Systems Update – iOSYou

You have probably accumulated a variety of tools and techniques you could apply to your own thoughts from the day-to-day actions that you so unconsciously execute with the interactions and engagements with your social media devices, apps and other media outlets you use. As you scroll from page to page, and swipe from profile to profile, the contents of your mind generally fills with thoughts that filter down to influence and shape the feelings and emotions that you experience within your body. Comparing yourself to others is all too easy. Having an opinion for something that doesn't relate to you or your own life is something that you probably do with great ease, and generally with very little effort. Passing judgement may have become natural to you and blocking those who don't float your boat is as simple as swiping left. These actions that you take so freely can also be applied to help improve the state of your own mind. With these everyday actions being so effortless and so natural, you generally don't hold a five-year grudge because someone didn't like your photo post; however, in your physical world, life can be a bit more complicated than that which goes on in your digital world. With your daily social actions being so repetitive, so normal and natural, why is it easy to block someone online, but then difficult to block them out of your mind? – Have you even tried?

You are always going to be a product of what you think you are. Your thoughts and beliefs are always going to shape and create your existence, and how you feel, and also how you see the world around you, how you interact with others and how you value yourself. The thoughts you have in your head will always direct the experiences that you have in your life, simply from the thoughts that you choose to think. In realising that you have limitless choices for the thoughts that you choose, you can now change the way that you experience your life for the better. Having self-control over the repetitive thoughts and inner conversations that contributes to the stomach-churning anxiety that washes over you, can seem like a major challenge for so many. There are also individuals who are unable to escape the fear in their mind from the tiniest spider, **who's actually probably more scared of the size of them.** Thinking and expecting the worst-case scenario may be an activity that you so easily and naturally engage in. Then there are the years of being overly self-critical and doubtful of yourself, perhaps that's what you personally do quite well? The limiting patterns and actions can go on and on; however, to me, it's clear that all of these situations and they'll be so many more that you may very easily do, **all originate in the mind**.

The operating functions of your mind are different from those that you live with. Yes, you will have similarities between the two, which is why you get on and match; however, the finer details of how you form and drive your experiences will differ to those that you share a couch with. Let's look closely at the point I'm making: **that you are *forming your experiences*.** You see, you probably think that the fear of flying is something that you have no control over. You may think that your bouts of anxiety are uncontrollable and unfair. As you feel the effects of your experiences and seek refuge from the eight-legged creatures that cause you to make sounds similar to Mariah Carey, let's really consider **the control room of your mind.**

Every app that you use and every piece of technology that you enjoy has a user manual that no one ever reads. You work things out for yourself. You switch things on, charge them up, enter your information, pout for your profile image, and everything is up and running. The food recipes that you follow are available with the step-by-step guidance that allows you to materialise, with great ease, end products to please your pallet. The playlists of Ariana are all too easy to find on YouTube, as are the videos of Madonna falling down the stairs. You have reached a point in your life where a Snickers bar can be delivered to your front door, and you can have a video call with someone on the other side of the world. It's all so easy.

The most complicated thing in your life is probably your mind and the thoughts that are obscuring the thinking that is going on inside yourself, which you probably don't think you are in control of. Wrong. **You're always in control.** You probably just haven't worked out how to edit the selfie of self-doubt that you hold so dearly of yourself. It just needs a new filter. The inner voice saying 'you're not good enough' may have been stuck on repeat since you were thirteen years old, along with the replay of the worst day of your life, which you've watched and talked about over and over again, leaving you to feel that it just won't go away. Well it can, and you probably don't believe me, but if you can filter a photo or scroll past something that you don't want to watch online, you can learn very easily and very quickly how to work the systems manual of your mind.

Why didn't they teach you this in school, you may wonder? Because Pythagoras's theorem was more important than the state of your mental and emotional health. So, as we get to work in looking at, to listening to and now understanding the feelings that you feel, the thoughts that you hear and think, we need first to get back to the control room of your mind.

Like anything in your life, practice and repetition is going to give you the strength in knowing how to do something really, really well. **Stalking other people on Instagram without them knowing, isn't something**

you mastered in a day. Making your dating profile sound perfect required great time and attention to detail. Mastering your mindset is easier than you think. Past pain, future worries – you name it – you can change it. **It all comes down to you taking control and allowing yourself to be patient.**

Your mental health is of great importance for you, and also for those you live with and those that you work with. It's generally good for the planet. You are not trying to be perfect and have it all together. **You are not trying to make your mind seem as perfect as a Kardashian Instagram profile.** You are going to experience the practicalities of your mind and your thoughts, and some of the elements of the operating system within that can and will work for you. You are going to now realise that you have more control, and that you can deal with problematic feelings and emotions better, as you now begin to understand the systems manual of your mind. In understanding that you have choices and options to operate, edit, eliminate, and update the ways in which your thoughts are being formed within your head in a variety of ways, you very powerfully put yourself in a position to stop any self-suffering. You can see this journey that you are now embarking on as a **'system's update' for your mind.** All apps and devices go through updates to iron out the bugs, the operations that are not working well, and they come back with improved and better versions of themselves. At times the same updates would do wonders for each individual, to recover from the bugs that have developed, to eliminate and improve the limiting functioning methods that aren't allowing you to thrive in your life, to change and transform things mentally and emotionally for the better.

When something is broken, we act so quickly to fix or replace it. We spend so much time setting up a new phone so that it operates well. **We could spend some time setting up our own minds as well.** Having an alert or an update that tells us things within need ironing out would be greatly beneficial, and yet that's exactly what your mind and body has been doing for you for so long. When you're stuck in a cycle of anxiety, your mind and body are talking to you. When emotionally you're suffering mentally, **something needs healing.** A systems update would be a perfect option and opportunity for you to turn your focus within, only **you would be acting out the service.** Instead of allowing yourself to remain stuck or suffering at the hands of your mind and your emotions, you can now begin to understand and experience the position that you can be in to have more mental and emotional self-relief.

Self-helping can lead to self-healing, self-knowing, and self-leading, as you begin to learn and understand that you can become the master of your own universe. This is an experience that you can have now. You can learn just how to cope with your thoughts and with your personal experiences. You can begin to overcome all that holds you back in your mind, and you can learn ways that will allow you to stand strong in your mind, as you come to now understand and experience **the power of your own mind.**

Allow yourself to be open to the ways that you know only too well that you engage with each and every day. **They can and will bring peace to your mind.** Discovering the various daily methods that you can apply to your mind that you use so freely and effortlessly to change what you're viewing online, is going to help transform the mental movies and mind mp3's that dominate your world within. Your opportunity to have resources that you activate in anytime and anyplace without anyone else knowing how you are directing the actions of your mind, will allow you to engulf any positive state that you need to bring peace to your mind. In your attempts now to understand that you hold the key position for who and how you are, you can now become active in freeing yourself from all that no longer serves you any positive purpose in your life. **Your time is now.** Your ability to know is right here. Your opportunity to thrive as you transform is all part of your own healing.

Disclaimer

Let me make some things clear for you. Your life challenges may have ripped you open to your core and you may have emotionally collapsed and mentally struggled to find the strength to rise back up to your feet. You may have suffered within from the self-torture of your thoughts, the things that you tell yourself, and the beliefs that you hold of yourself, or that others have installed into your perception of the world. However life has been for you, **I want you to take several deep breaths.** I want you to allow your mind to now open to the possibilities that you can now elicit into your life, through your mind, as you begin to explore ways that help you in your life and as you begin to work on your internal experiences. As you begin to look past your challenges, and as you now come to step away from the worries that tremor through your mind, I ask you to be open to trying, to receiving and experiencing the self-changes that you, yourself can create. However difficult life may have been for you and however hard times may have tested you, try not to underestimate the effects that are possible from the work that you can now experience. The simple actions that you take on a daily basis can and will help bring mental and emotional relief within you. Allow yourself to feel the benefits of such normal and natural actions that you execute on a daily basis, which can help with the state of your own mind. The processes that follow may work immediately or you may have to <u>repeat</u> them to make sure that you have understood them or so that you can continue to keep them strong. <u>Repetition may be key</u>. **You can't expect to run a marathon without any training.** Think of this as a 'mind work out', the more reps that you do, the stronger the actions can then become for you to activate and implement them, as and when you need to. Do not listen to any doubts; do not pay attention to any resistance.

Imagine yourself removing a tree from the ground where the roots are so tough and strong. A tremendous amount of effort may be required at the beginning; however, you can see this opportunity now as a space for you to remove the unwanted and to now plant seeds of strength that can grow into your life – seeds of hope, love, joy, relief, strength, power, control and so much more.

🏠 What would you like to grow in the space of your mind?

🏠 What would feel more comfortable to be surrounded with in your thoughts?

🏠 Is it time to let more light inside the home of your mind?

Allow yourself to notice any changes that you experience. Your symptoms may reduce and may still be there in a lower strength. Acknowledge the changes, not just the weakened feeling that remains. Notice all progress where you can. In some cases, change will be immediate, and you will feel overjoyed by the freedom that you feel. Then what? Fear not. All that consumed you, that will have then left you, now leaves space for new growth, new strength, and better ways of living.

Lessons for integrating the rest of your life with your new mind tools so that your sense of control gets easier and stronger each day, follows in the final section of this book. But for now, **let me introduce you to your Digital Mind.**

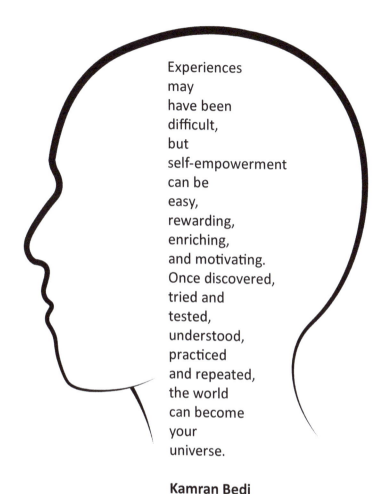

Experiences
may
have been
difficult,
but
self-empowerment
can be
easy,
rewarding,
enriching,
and motivating.
Once discovered,
tried and
tested,
understood,
practiced
and repeated,
the world
can become
your
universe.

Kamran Bedi

Chapter 4

Your Digital Mind

With practice, perseverance, and patience, healthy and natural life changing habits can be formed and integrated into your daily life.

*Allow yourself to explore the following methods as you step inside your mind. Experiment on the content that you edit. **Persevere and have patience**. Choose one particular method at a time and give each option an experience. You may find one works instantly for you, and for others you may need to apply them several times. Follow the instructions as you now come to understand how you can take control of your mind.*

Too Many Tabs

A noisy mind, a chaotic mind, an angry mind, a worried mind, an anxious mind and a heavy mind can prove difficult to live in.

- 🏠 How many **tabs** do you have open in your mind?

- 🏠 How many different windows of thought are you looking at that are causing you to feel mentally and emotionally strained in your physical body?

- 🏠 Do you have **tabs** from the past open?

- 🏠 Are there windows of thoughts open for your future?

- 🏠 What is happening inside your mind with your thoughts?

You may have carelessly closed tab after tab, window after window on the digital appliances that you use each and every day. Imagine if your tablets, laptops, and your phones had **tabs** open that represented memories of your past or even visions of anxiety for your future. Would you sit and watch them or even keep them open on your technological screens, or would you move your mouse or your finger to the **X** to close the **tabs** and windows?

🏠 How would you feel if someone walked past and saw what **tabs** and windows you had open, in relation to your personal thoughts being shown on an external screen?

🏠 'Why are you still replaying the movie of your ex from five years ago', a friend may ask?

🏠 'Are you seriously sitting watching that montage of plane crashes weeks before you're meant to fly', a colleague may question?

If all of these actions of self-viewing, and self-consumption are actions that you would not engage with in your outer world, why would you let them happen on repeat in your inner world?

Leo was an extremely talented and successful TV personality (of course, I've changed his name) who came into my practice for his first session with me with his laptop open. Leo had emails coming in, Facebook posts he was scheduling, photos he was filtering, his website he was blogging on, YouTube open, holidays he was planning and so much more. As we got to work on his outcomes, one of the issues Leo was having was that he felt burnt out. He felt exhausted mentally, and in his own words, his mind felt heavy, noisy, busy, and tired, which he felt he just couldn't control. He'd tried meditating and practising yoga; however, his mind remained distracted and consumed, even during those practices. He even found it difficult to start his appointment with me on time as his focus was on the busy windows and **tabs** that were open on his laptop screen. Having discussed various areas of his life, I invited him to relax as I encouraged him to breathe, to close his eyes, and to step inside the home of his mind.

K - 'Tell me what's going on inside your mind.'

It took Leo some time.

L – 'It's so busy' 'I can't make it out, as there's just so much flowing through my head for so much that's going on in my life.'

K – 'From what you see inside, are there any thought images or mini mental movies?'.

L –'Some are movies some are single thoughts.'

K - 'Look now at the content in your mind as **tabs** that are open, just as you have on your own laptop. See them as different **tabs** on the screen of your mind, with different content showing?'.

L – 'Yes' there's so many **tabs** that I've got open.'

K –'How many **tabs**? Take your time. Count how many **tabs** you can now see.'

After a long pause Leo answered, 'over twenty.'

K – 'With your mind, mentally close the **tabs** that you see open as you would on your laptop, do this now quite quickly. Close them all down so that you make them disappear one by one until your screen within is clear.'

Leo took his time and for some **tabs** he found it difficult to close. For others, he found that they disappeared with great ease. What surprised him was that he found there were **tabs** that were open in the home of his mind for a relationship he had been in three years ago. In the process of closing the **tabs**, Leo felt a sense of peace within himself and also lighter in his mind, where he acknowledged the peace he felt mentally, which encouraged his body to relax.

When you begin to look at the **tabs** and windows that are open in your mind, you'll notice that they can change on a daily basis, and also with circumstance for where you are and whom you're with. You can begin to notice just how busy your mind is. You may have so many **tabs** open, even with some that go back so many years, which, without your awareness, are then causing you to feel in a particularly negative way within yourself. I've had people tell me that they wake up at 3am most nights as they have so much 'going on' in their minds, leaving them like zombies as they struggle through their day-to-day activities. You may be aware that the more **tabs** that are open on your laptop, tablets, and phones, the more the battery gets used up and drained down. Can you see how your mind with so many **tabs** open could be taking up so much of your physical energy?

A busy mind with an internal screen full of various open **tabs** may leave you feeling unpleasant and uncomfortable feelings, even at times when you're happy. If you have several **tabs** open, your focus and your energy are going to be split between the **tabs** of content in your mind that you're then viewing, distracting you from the ease of each present moment. You may have several **tabs** open or maybe just one tab open for one person or one experience that dominates your screen within. As you look now at how easy it is to close something online that you don't want to watch or see, like one of those Facebook videos that just opens and plays without you wanting to see it, you know you can simply press close and you've taken the action to make it disappear. No matter if it's an image that makes you feel uncomfortable, a song that you don't want to hear, or a video clip that you don't want to watch, you can simply press close and take more control over the actions of your mind.

<u>Let's press close on the tabs that are open and active in your mind.</u>

In a comfortable position, choose now whether to close your eyes or keep them open, (whichever works best for you) and step inside the home of your mind. Some of the tabs may be open closer to you, others may be far away or even layered covering other tabs like pop ups, or you may have them neatly in order. They may be in colour or black and white. Some may be moving, playing, or still images and you may even hear some sounds. When you are ready, step in and see the tabs that are open. Take your time and with your mind acting like a control panel, press close on the tabs. See the tabs disappear from the space within until all tabs are closed and then take notice of how you feel. If any tabs reopen or pop up, close them again. Repeat the actions as you would on any of your devices and do it quickly. Close all the tabs that are not serving you any positive purpose in your mind and notice how it feels when they are gone. Notice the sounds disappear and also notice the space that opens up in the space of your mind. If they pop open again, immediately close them out of sight.

<u>Step by step actions:</u>

1. Step inside the home of your mind.

2. See what you see: notice the tabs or windows that you have open. Take your time.

3. **Begin to press X and close the tabs in your mind.**

4. **Make them disappear with ease as you press close.**

5. **Repeat until all tabs and windows are closed, and if and when any others pop up in your mind, close them.**

6. **Try to close them quickly.**

7. **Notice the changes.**

8. **Try this method a few times. Should you need, repeat the process 1-6 times to allow the process to experience its full effect.**

9. **Use this procedure often and when necessary.**

Repeat. *Have patience.* Repeat. *Build control.* Repeat. *Have patience.* Repeat. *Notice the difference to the state of your mind.*

By taking control of your mind, and stepping into your personal space, you allow yourself to close the **tabs** of the content that consumes you within, no matter if they are past **tabs**, present **tabs**, future **tabs,** or any **tabs**. Simply close what you do not need in the home of your mind. Allow yourself now to mentally relieve your mind and your emotions, and to feel the positive difference to your physical body as you update and tidy up the space you experience within.

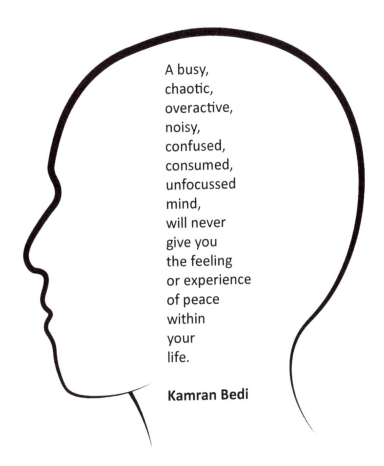

A busy,
chaotic,
overactive,
noisy,
confused,
consumed,
unfocussed
mind,
will never
give you
the feeling
or experience
of peace
within
your
life.

Kamran Bedi

Press STOP

You can end up playing the same old memories, conversations, scenes, and scenarios from your past, or projections for your future over and over in your mind. Your present and current experiences that bother you and challenge you, can end up overly consuming you, as they become the current trending topics that fill the space within your thoughts. Listening in on the content that plays out within and watching the same painful memories or the fearful future projections that cause you anxiety can take its toll on your mind and your emotions. Having an over active mind where the next episode just plays without you wanting it to can make you feel like your mind is stuck on repeat. You can end up losing sleep, missing out on the ease of the present moment, feeling stressed, being consumed with worry – all from the actions that play out inside your head.

Whether it's online or at home, the screens that you tend to watch and listen in on are always your choice. Ok, you may be forced into watching *Match Of The Day* or *Love Island*, but you can control and choose what plays out in your mind. Instead of being overly consumed by what you allow to dominate your world within, you can take control by closing the **tabs** on the screens and sounds within. You can powerfully reduce the action in your mind by pressing **STOP**.

Thoughts, mental movies and inner conversations can go around and round inside your head, playing out the pains of your past, the fears of tomorrow, and a constant cycle of self-criticism. If you give power, space, and air time to worry, that's what will dominate you emotionally. Learning to take control – and most importantly – choosing to switch off, can give you instant mental and emotional relief.

It was school exam season in the UK and sat before me with her mother was an overwhelmed and over worried fifteen-year-old. The teen's overactive mind which was focussed on the pressure of her exams, was feeling the strain of her internal world. (*underlined words highlight the internal experience being had*) 'I can't stop thinking about the exams', 'I keep telling myself that I don't know enough', 'I'm fearing that I'll fail'. The language said it all. This bright youngster was running negative mental movies and thoughts of her exams on repeat. It was internal chatter that she didn't know enough, which led to the feelings of fear that produced thoughts and internal talk of potential failure. Having slowed her frantic and panicked pace down, so that she was in a more resourceful place to operate her mind, I introduced her to the remote control of her mind. In pressing **STOP** on the thoughts and sounds in her mind, she was able to bring the action on the screens within to a standstill. With the scenes and sounds now paused, it was a perfect opportunity to then close down these **tabs**. I encouraged her to then sit in the self-created free, quiet, and still space of her mind, and gave her the opportunity to as and when needed press **STOP** again, to **STOP** the characters within from playing out their fearful and worrying scenes.

In realising that you have the power to control the people, places, sounds, and content that perform on loop in your mind, you can take the control panel of your mind – whether it be a remote control, a touch screen or a control room – and you can choose to **STOP** the action inside your own head.

🏠 Would the **STOP** function help you reduce the activity in your mind as you lay in bed?

🏠 How would the **STOP** button make a difference to you thinking over what's yet to happen, or as you replay the events of the past?

Let's press STOP on the scenes and sounds that are playing out within.

Imagine that you have a remote control or touch screen that controls the settings of your mind. If you feel that imagining is difficult for you or if you think that it's silly, just remind yourself of the worst-case scenarios that you've imagined in the space of your own thoughts. Your mind's ability to do exactly what you tell it to do is available, so as I was saying, imagine now a remote control or touch screen that

controls your mind. On that screen or remote control see a button vividly in your mind that has the word written STOP. Build up a representation of this STOP button and mentally keep it in the same space and place in your mind. Really make it vivid. If it helps, give it a colour and create a feeling for how it feels to touch the button in your mind. Know that this button is there for you to press STOP on, as and when you need it to STOP the scenes that play out within and that also STOP the sounds, conversations, and self-talk that may be causing you any emotional distress.

Alternatively, just press STOP if it's easier for you to do so without imagining the STOP button.

Step by step actions:

1. Having built up a representation of your STOP button, use it often.

2. Use your awareness and notice when you're stuck in a cycle of negative thoughts, difficult thoughts, critical self-talk, repeats of what others said – all in the space of your mind. Notice when your mind is running at 100mph when you're trying to fall asleep. Notice when your mind is overactive with action when you're feeling anxious.

3. Press STOP. See the scenes STOP; hear the sounds STOP; make everything you need to STOP, STOP!

4. Having stopped everything, notice everything slow down and become calmer.

5. If it kicks off again in your mind, press STOP.

6. Activate the button as often as you need and bring your attention to the present place. (a further step and guidance of being more present is coming up) But for now, get used to using STOP.

7. Try this method a few times. Should you need, repeat the process 1-6 times to allow the process to experience its full effect.

8. Use this procedure often and when necessary.

Repeat. *Have patience.* Repeat. *Build control.* Repeat. *Have patience.* Repeat. *Notice the difference to the state of your mind.*

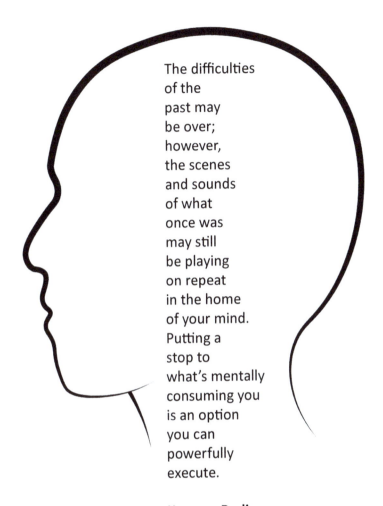

The difficulties
of the
past may
be over;
however,
the scenes
and sounds
of what
once was
may still
be playing
on repeat
in the home
of your mind.
Putting a
stop to
what's mentally
consuming you
is an option
you can
powerfully
execute.

Kamran Bedi

Empty Your Trash

Did you know that every time you access a memory, you change it? You may spend a lot of time thinking about what happened in your past, or you may have thoughts that pop up and play over in your mind as they visit you, often without you personally inviting them in. In your recollection of playing the memories through your mind, you can end up distorting the memories that you have in a variety of ways. You can, in fact even change the meaning of the memories without even realising it. Your current environment, the situations in your life, and your day-to-day mood can always influence your mind. As you time travel back through the time capsule of your mind to re-watch and re-feel what was and what happened, you could be influencing the memory negatively from the way that you currently feel. The environment that you're in as well as the perception that you choose to take, can also influence this. Any of these factors can strengthen and even distort the reality that you now perceive, sometimes making the memory worse. You may think of a situation that happened in your mind and feel angry about it, when at the time you may have actually felt disappointed. The memory that was laid down in your mind at the time could have been for example; disappointment, which could now be overridden by the reflective action you take in looking back, where you now feel anger and add anger to your memory. So, as you think back, now feeling angry for the disappointment you once felt, you potentially associate anger to the memory and change the way it is formed within, which you then contribute to your own personal suffering. This can happen time after time and with so many different and uncomfortable memories – all from the time that you spend playing the memories over and over.

🏠 Does time spent in your mind thinking about what was or what happened and lacing those memories with how you presently feel about the past situation help you in any particular way?

🏠 What could you do to make things easier in your mind?

🏠 Why not mentally close the **tabs** or press **STOP**?

Another way you can access mental and emotional relief alongside closing down your mental **tabs** and pressing **STOP**, is through another action that you use each and every day, which involves emptying your **trash**. You will throw things away without holding on to those possessions without thinking and with great ease. **You will so freely let go of what no longer serves you.** You wouldn't carry around piles and cases of **trash** from what you didn't need, from what's not serving you in your life each and every day, from moment to moment, everywhere that you went. Letting go is an action you do every day. You choose so carelessly and so freely to let go of what you no longer need. Here is another way you can work with the contents of your mind.

🏠 Can you recall moving things into the **trash** on a laptop or tablet? You drag the image, document and item across your screen and drop it down in the corner into the **trash**?

🏠 Perhaps you can hear the sounds and recall the times when you've dropped bottles into your outside bin?

On your digital devices, as you released the items into the **trash,** you may have heard the sound of glass breaking as it fell into the **trash**, or you may have heard the sound of paper being scrunched up as a piece of **trash**? Imagine hearing some of those sounds **now** in your mind. Hear the clear sounds of glass breaking in the **trash** or paper being scrunched up and repeat it a few more times, to make the sound really clear within your own head. Make the sound as loud as you need to for yourself.

Now you have the option to close the **tabs** in your mind and to press **STOP** – and now you can mentally find your own **trash** to empty out and clear the **trash** that's not serving you in positive ways within your mind.

<u>Drag, drop, release, and let go.</u>

Use this action in your mind to take hold of the thoughts and sounds that dominate the space within and then drag them to your trash. Let your trash basket be down in the bottom right corner of the screen and space within your mind, really far down low in the corner. Then drag your content down to that corner and drop it into the trash, allowing yourself to hear the sounds of your content entering the trash basket and shattering into pieces like glass. As you release it, let go of it and allow yourself to feel the space within, and to see the screen in your mind to be then clear. You should feel open and free of what was dominating the space you now look in on.

<u>Step by step actions:</u>

1. **Locate the memory, the item, the file, the image, the sound, or the feeling that's bothering you.**

2. **Using the control panel of your mind, get a hold of it and drag it towards your mental trash basket, which should be located at the bottom right hand of your mental screen.**

3. **Mentally drop the item in your trash and hear the sounds you associate with the item falling into the trash. (glass breaking, or paper being screwed up, or a sound that works for you)**

4. **Tidy up the home of your mind and put anything that no longer needs to be there into the trash.**

5. **Encourage yourself to get rid of negative feelings, difficult sounds, thoughts, or movies from the past, present, or future that are bothering you by dragging them to the trash.**

6. **Do this action again quickly, repeating it where necessary.**

7. **Try this method a few times. Should you need, repeat the process 1-6 times to allow the process to experience its full effect.**

8. **Use this procedure often and when necessary.**

Repeat. *Have patience.* Repeat. *Build control.* Repeat. *Have patience.* Repeat. *Notice the difference to the state of your mind.*

You may find pressing **STOP** on the content, the memory, or even the person that dominates the space within will help you then grab a hold of it so you can take it to the **trash**. The more that you choose to remove the items in your mind that are showing up and distracting and disturbing you mentally and emotionally, the more control you will build up to execute these actions with more relief and ease, in any given moment. Give this a try now. Before you read any further, locate something in your mind that you want to feel free from, and drag it over, and drop it in your **trash** basket. It may take a while to get a hold of the item and it may slip away from you. Practice and repeat. Take control and empty out, from your mind, all that is no longer serving you.

As with your mental **tabs**, your **STOP** button, and now with clearing away the content that you don't need in your mind, go as slowly or quickly as necessary, and repeat as often as required.

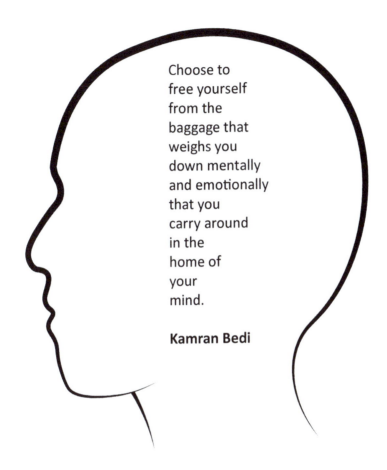

Choose to
free yourself
from the
baggage that
weighs you
down mentally
and emotionally
that you
carry around
in the
home of
your
mind.

Kamran Bedi

Swipe or BLOCK

I believe the <u>BLOCK</u> function is available pretty much everywhere: Facebook, Twitter, Instagram, Snapchat, Grindr, and Tinder. You can even <u>BLOCK</u> a contact, an email address or a cold caller – all gone in a second. The power of a button can make things **STOP**, disappear, and not have any impact in your life. You can choose to <u>BLOCK</u> someone out of your life so freely and easily. How good would it feel to <u>BLOCK</u> the person out of your mind?

You will also naturally <u>BLOCK</u> so many things out of your sight and in your sounds on a day-to-day basis. You don't look at every face on the tube or train; you don't see every car that drives past you – your mind automatically blocks out specific information as you choose what you want to focus on.

'He blocked me on Grindr', a friend said. 'She blocked me on Facebook following my anti-Brexit views', said another friend. 'I've blocked my ex from seeing my Instagram content', a friend told a friend. 'Blocking' is a now normal and natural action that provides an immediate and instant result – blocking further contact or sharing, or consumption of information.

Think about the blocking actions that you yourself have taken in your life. Think of the number of times that you may have used this on a cold caller, on a follower, or on a dating site to get away from persistent messaging or undesired behaviour.

🏠 What's popping up in your mind that's distracting you?

🏠 How are you allowing the faces or mental movies of what once was to disturb your inner joy and peace?

The amount of time that you spend scrolling and swiping each and every day on the news feeds and timelines of your favourite apps gives you another immediate and effective action alongside <u>BLOCK</u> that you can apply to the news feed and timeline of your own thoughts.

🏠 How often do you just **SWIPE** away content that you don't want to view, listen to or consume?

🏠 How easy is it to **SWIPE** something out of your view and how often are you swiping your external screens on phones, tablets, and laptops each and every day?

Technically, on the dating app Tinder, if you **SWIPE** right to an image and a profile, you are generally saying 'yes' to the information that you are viewing. Swiping left, however, is an immediate 'no'. That means the person is gone, dusted, and extinguished all from the site of your own eyes. This immediate swiping action to scroll content out of view, to move your news feed or timeline away from what you don't want to view, and on to all that you do want to know about, is again, a repetitive and daily choice that you take each and every day.

Whether it's difficult thoughts, difficult memories, people's faces popping up in your mind, or even worries and fears for the future, you can take action and <u>BLOCK</u> out all that no longer serves you any positive purpose in your life. You can also attempt to SWIPE the content of your mind away from your personal screen within to feel an immediate and effective shift.

SWIPE or <u>BLOCK</u>, here's how to take action.

<u>Steps by step actions to BLOCK:</u>

1. **Mentally form an image in your mind of a deep RED lettered word with the word BLOCK written.**

2. **Make this stretch to fill the screen of your mind so that you only see the red word BLOCK. Let it be written over a complete black screen so the red letters are on top of a black screen, which you are stretching out so you only see the letters and a black screen. When it pops up, it covers the content you are choosing to BLOCK.**

3. **When you need to find mental relief, make the image in your mind, the movie playing,**

the person who you can't get out of your head, or the situation that is playing on repeat and then imagine it covered in your BLOCK screen.

4. Allow your screen within to very quickly and at a fast speed pop up the image BLOCK and black out anything else so that all you see is the red letters and black background in your mind.

5. Repeat this quickly over and over until the image or mental movie that is bothering you does not appear anymore.

6. Try pressing STOP first if needed and then apply the BLOCK pop up at least 5 times over the person, memory, or content in your mind, making it stronger and stronger in order to make the content behind the BLOCK weaker and less accessible.

7. Try this method a few times. Should you need, repeat the process 1-6 times to allow the process to experience its full effect.

8. Use this procedure often and when necessary.

<u>Steps by step actions to SWIPE:</u>

1. **Simply move the content in your mind out of view.**

2. **Swipe it all to one side until it disappears off the screen of your mind.**

3. **Swipe it so far away that you can't see it anymore.**

4. **Scroll down to something better and less consuming.**

5. **Swipe away any thoughts, images of people, past, or future content that may be on the screen within.**

6. **Try this method a few times. Should you need, repeat the process 1-6 times to allow the process to experience its full effect.**

7. Use this procedure often and when necessary.

<u>Repeat</u>. *Have patience.* <u>Repeat</u>. *Build control.* <u>Repeat</u>. *Have patience.* <u>Repeat</u>. *Notice the difference to the state of your mind.*

The key here is to act fast and to repeat these actions in your mind as quickly as you would on a digital screen to change the content that you view within for the better.

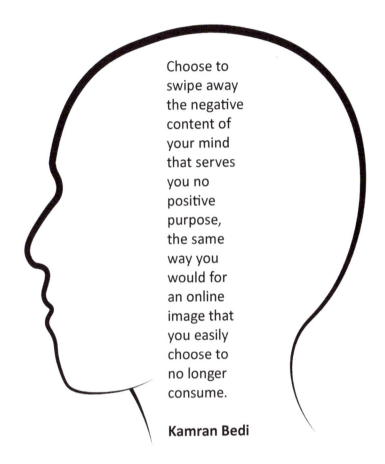

Choose to
swipe away
the negative
content of
your mind
that serves
you no
positive
purpose,
the same
way you
would for
an online
image that
you easily
choose to
no longer
consume.

Kamran Bedi

Filter

In your perfect online world, everything gets filtered and edited where you have the choice to delete the bad and to showcase the good, all from choice. You get to scroll and **SWIPE** away from anything you don't like, you can close windows and **tabs**, <u>BLOCK</u> out people and trolls, and even unfollow anything that bothers you or doesn't interest you. The screen within your mind doesn't have to be a news feed of difficult past images or mental movies that are flowing through the timeline of your mind. You can now also use the same actions to filter the content that you no longer want to view or be a part of, for past, present, and even future-based scenarios that may be dominating your space within. Filtering out your internal content as you do so easily and effortlessly with your online content can immediately change and transform the meaning and feelings associated with all that you view. Various quick intervention techniques from the NLP world that I use with my clients help to change and transform the meaning of an experience, with great speed leading to an immediate positive impact. Using filters to work on the internal representation of an experience can and does change the feelings associated with the images, mental movies, or memories. In choosing now to use filters in the same way you would to change the content you post online, can also be applied to change the content that fills the screen within your mind.

There are filters available on nearly all social media platforms. You can so easily change the style, the lighting, and your appearance. Your skin can look flawless, your life can appear glamourous – all from filtering out what you consider to be 'bad'. On many applications including Snapchat and on the Instastory, you can very easily choose to add a filter, which turns you into a rabbit, leaving you with bunny ears, or a dog where a cartoon tongue extends out of your mouth as you talk. You can even manipulate the tone, sound, and impact of the words that you speak. These filter options, which are continually changing and updating, give you with the choice to change the experience that is viewed. The feelings are generally feel good feelings, as the image or clips becomes distorted from what is really the reality. Having the ability to filter out the images and movies in your mind, to change their appearances, the sounds you hear, the words, and how they are said by applying different filters can change how you feel within yourself about the content that fills your mind.

This process worked particularly well with a sixteen-year-old male client who was experiencing anxiety and panic. Feeling nervous and apprehensive about his future, because he had been bullied in his past, he was nervous about moving forward with his life into a new college. One of his main interests was Snapchat, where he showed me how exactly it worked as well as why he enjoyed using it. He explained how he liked using the lenses and filters and how sending them to friends or putting them on to his story with more of a comical, relaxed and happy feel was uplifting and enjoyable to watch. As he was using this feature on such a regular basis, like so many other people, I asked him to tell me what was on the screen of his mind. He informed me of his internal news feed, which was in relation to the individuals who had bullied him. He replied that he could see their faces and hear the words that they had said to him and that he couldn't get them out of his head. This led him to then play future-based scenes and scenarios in his mind where there were other people doing the same actions in his new college. I asked him when you imagine this happening; 'do you have a picture'? he replied yes *'it's of people bullying me'*. I immediately said put a filter on all of their faces and turn them into rabbits. He laughed as he did this, and the feeling he had instantly changed; the bullies he imagined now seemed less intimidating. *'Make them have rabbit's teeth in your mind, with floppy ears and twitching noses and as you do that, make the image of them in your mind smaller, like the size of a passport photo'*, I instructed. So, in his head he had filtered the image, changed them to rabbits and resized them, making them very small. He then reported he had no feelings of overwhelm or intimidation. He was also able to do this with ease as I had guided him to make use of the actions that he was already using on a daily basis with so much ease.

He could now use these filters in the 'make-up' of his own mind. He instantly distorted the content within and took control over how it appeared on the screen within. I then instructed him to find the image of the past bullies as we had worked on the imagined future image he was creating for his new college that was causing him anxiety. On the past image I instructed him to also filter their appearance in his mind and to write over their rabbit faced, passport photo sized image in his mind, OVER in capitalized bolded letters. This was a reminder that this picture was in his past and he now had his future to create, and his present moment didn't have to include worry about what could potentially be. There was one last place this past image was moved to. I introduced him to his own personal **trash** basket and there he dragged and dropped the past image. When he released it, he heard the sound of breaking glass, which he could associate with letting go of the mental domination that it was having over him.

He did ask about what to do if the thoughts came back, a typical 'What if' situation which highlights anxiety. I then showed him how to close down any mind **tabs**, to BLOCK out any thoughts he didn't need, and to use his mind and his senses to be more mindful and more present, and less occupied in his mind.

Filters are fun and simple to use. They can take the edge off things and make it so easy to use to change and distort the images, movies, and sounds that we play within the news feeds and timelines of our minds.

Think about how you could apply different filters in your mind as you may do very easily in your day-to-day life, to change, and in most cases, improve, the images and posts that you put out online.

🏠 What could you make darker so that you can't see it as clearly?

🏠 What could you add a mask to, to <u>BLOCK</u> out, or change the image of a face you don't want to see?

🏠 Who could you turn into a rabbit, a dog, or a cat that then sounds pathetic, quieter and less dominant within your own mind?

<u>Step by step actions:</u>

1. **Locate an image of someone that sticks in your mind.**

2. **Make the image of the person's face still so it's not playing, a still image.**

3. **Filter the person, turn him into something else, apply a mask, change how she appears in your mind.**

4. **Turn the person upside down.**

5. **Write something bold over their image.**

6. **Make the image small; shrink it down.**

7. Place it in your trash.

8. Try this method a few times. Should you need, repeat the process 1-6 times to allow the process to experience its full effect.

9. Use this procedure often and when necessary.

Second option for filters:

1. Hear the sounds in your mind.

2. Notice the conversations, the things that you or others say in your personal space.

3. If something bothers you, filter it.

4. Change the tone – make the sounds appear like a cat talking or a mouse.

5. Check within to see if the words still have power over you?

6. Make the sounds seem like a small boy or small girl talking slowly.

7. Work with changing the sounds and tones and turn the volume down in your mind to zero!

8. Try this method a few times. Should you need, repeat the process 1-6 times to allow the process to experience its full effect.

9. Use this procedure often and when necessary.

Repeat. *Have patience.* Repeat. *Build control.* Repeat. *Have patience.* Repeat. *Notice the difference to the state of your mind.*

In realising that you can use the control panel of your mind to change, edit and filter the content that bothers you within, you can very easily take your power back and improve how you feel mentally and emotionally within yourself.

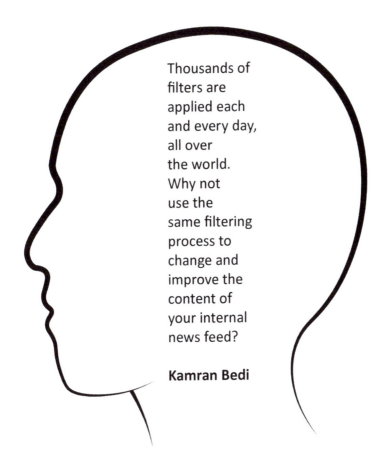

Thousands of
filters are
applied each
and every day,
all over
the world.
Why not
use the
same filtering
process to
change and
improve the
content of
your internal
news feed?

Kamran Bedi

Mute

The sounds within your own head can be detrimental to the ways you choose to live your life. You can have a variety of different inner voices; some that are your own, and range from happy to sad, worry to joy, fear, and even panic. There are also other voices in your mind that are those of people that you know. The ever-changing world of your timeline of mental movies, images, and conversations can change and evolve from day-to-day, place to place, and with each and every experience. Some internal sounds can be dominant at certain times, then lay dormant in the background and then pop back up to remind you of their annoyance.

- Perhaps you can identify and notice some of the things that are said in your head?

- Maybe there's a playlist of tracks, conversations, internal dialogue, or experiences that play over, as if on repeat?

You may feel as if there are sounds that you just can't get away from, voices and conversations that play over and over, the things you should have said, the words that hurt you, mixed and blended into the home of your mind.

I often suggest as a simple technique, to get a clearer understanding of what is being said by an individual to themselves or even by themselves **to verbally**

communicate out aloud the things they say to themselves in their own head. The way that you talk to yourself – the things that you say to yourself will always influence how you see the world, how you act and behave, and how you live your life all from the choices that you make. Just think about the things that you may be saying to yourself, and if you feel you are in a comfortable space to do so, **say them out loud.** You could say out loud the words that you hear other people saying to you, or have said to you, so again you can hear them out aloud again.

🏠 How do these words sound to you?

🏠 What do you hear?

🏠 Would you allow someone else to say the things that you say to yourself to other people?

🏠 Would you allow yourself to say the things that you said to yourself to other people?

People often have a lot of self-doubt, worry, and fear going through their minds. There's also the inner talk of 'I'm not worthy enough' or 'I'm not good enough', which can again have a negative mental and emotional impact on how you live your life. If you hear these conversations within, say them out loud.

🏠 Notice how it feels to really hear these words. Is it serving you any positive purpose?

🏠 Now think about this: If you are doing this in your head, chances are the people that you know, love, and care for are at times doing it inside their own heads. Would this cause you concern?

🏠 If your son, or daughter, friend or colleague was talking to themselves in their own head saying things like, 'I'm not good enough', 'I'm not worthy enough' how would that make you feel?

🏠 Is there any benefit for talking to yourself like that in your own head?

So many individuals that I've worked with and even conversed with across social media have difficult and negative inner voices that hinder their mental and emotional states. In talking about these things out aloud, you can gain some perspective and understanding that this type of talk just doesn't belong in your head.

🏠 Can you think of someone in your life who perhaps has an inner voice where there is completely no doubt?

🏠 A voice that they say in their head or that talks dominantly with confidence and certainty?

🏠 Can you think of someone in your life whose mental dialogue is generally geared toward procrastination?

🏠 They may have spent years thinking over what to do with their life, how they are going to do it, all the while talking themselves out of taking action and having results?

You can see how the inner voice can change from day to day and from experience to experience. I have had the experience of working with people who have had the inner voice of a parent, a teacher, a partner, and also a colleague stuck in their head, playing on repeat. The words and sounds have been negative; usually expressing their beliefs, which dominated and captured the way the individuals lived their lives.

🏠 How would it feel to have more control over the sounds that ring out from within?

🏠 Would it be better for you to be able to stop having the conversations over and over that consume you mentally and emotionally?

Steps by step actions:

1. **Notice the voices and sounds in your head.**

2. **Ask yourself how is the voice helping or hindering you?**

3. **Take the control panel of your mind.**

4. **Press MUTE.**

5. **Silence the sounds within.**

6. **Use your MUTE button as often as you require.**

7. **MUTE the sounds until you hear only silence.**

8. **Try this method a few times. Should you need, repeat the process 1-6 times to allow the process to experience its full effect.**

9. **Use this procedure often and when necessary.**

Repeat. *Have patience.* Repeat. *Build control.* Repeat. *Have patience.* Repeat. *Notice the difference to the state of your mind.*

This particular process works well by imagining that, in the control panel of your mind, you have a control button or remote control that you can just hit the **MUTE** button on. If there is a person, a conversation, or a voice that bothers you, simply and quickly hit **MUTE** to create the silence in your own mind. You could then use a filter to change their internal and now muted image, or close down the **tab** of their silent image or mini-movie that is open in your mind. When recently working with a regular client on FaceTime named Linda, Linda and I also used the visualisation of the volume 'off' symbol which appears on a phone when you turn the phone to silent. This visual representation is another option that you could integrate into your **MUTE** function of your Digital Mind.

esc

You can end up spending so much time in your mind, replaying yesterday or fretting about the prospects of tomorrow, that it can drain you mentally and emotionally, dragging you away from the ease of the present moment. As you rattle around the home of your mind and float in and out of the present moment going back and forth from thoughts in your head to your physical environment, you can end up spending more time in your head than in your physical space. As I previously said, memories can be changed, edited and influenced from the times that we spend accessing our past thoughts. You can also end up building up problems, situations, and scenarios that negatively affect your mental and emotional health, from the time you spend thinking through your thoughts. **Most of the things that you spend time thinking about may never actually happen.** On your commute to work, out at a dinner, and even lying in bed as you attempt to fall asleep, the thoughts in your internal and private space can end up disturbing your inner peace.

Learning to be more present, to be mindful of not only your thoughts but also of the space that you're in mentally – whether it's deep in your thoughts or fully in the present moment – can help you not to be overly disturbed by the content of your mind. It is in the present moment where life can be easier for you. You can be less fearful and experience a sense of peace.

The **esc** button on a laptop, tablet or computer can bring you out of the places that you digitally no longer want to be in. You also have other buttons that provide the same relief and exit in your digital world. For example, the side button on your phone that clicks, can close your phone off and turn the screen black. The centre button on some phones closes an app, a video, an image and returns to the home screen.

🏠 How could you return to the home of your physical body to be in the place that you're physically in and not in the traffic of your mind?

🏠 Could you **esc** and step mentally into the present moment, to join your physical body in the place that you're in to find mental and emotional relief?

<u>Steps to take actions:</u>

1. **Stop getting caught up in your thoughts.**

2. **Use your awareness to realise where you're spending the most time. Are you in the living room of your mind or in your own physical space?**

3. **Tap your first finger and thumb together and release, as if you were pressing a button.**

4. **As you do it, mentally see the word or say the word esc (escape) and bring yourself out of your mind.**

5. **Tap your thumb and finger and esc. You may need to do it a few times to snap out of your thoughts and the state that you are in.**

6. **Use your eyes to see the space around you. Hear the sounds in your environment, feel the temperature and fabrics of your clothes on your skin. Step fully into the present moment.**

7. **Try this method a few times. Should you need, repeat the process 1-6 times to allow the process to experience its full effect.**

8. **Use this procedure often and when necessary.**

Repeat. *Have patience.* Repeat. *Build control.* Repeat. *Have patience.* Repeat. *Notice the difference to the state of your mind.*

With this particular technique, you are using your thumb and finger – or you could even tap your foot on the floor – at the same time, say **esc** (escape) in your mind or out loud or remind yourself of **esc** to come out of your mind. The physical movement of your thumb and finger, (or tapping your foot) tied with a visual of the word **esc** or by verbally saying **esc** can make a stronger link and association in your mind to step out of the home of your mind, and to be more mentally and emotionally present.

Updating Your Internal System

All of these actions that you can make with your mind can be done in any place and any moment **without anyone else knowing that you are doing them.** You can create a better mental and emotional experience for yourself in your mind and body, without declaring what you are doing. You can very quickly take your power, and you can change and transform things for yourself for the better. The more that you practice and repeat these techniques, the easier and more effective they will become for you in your life. You can choose one or more in particular that works for you. Allow yourself time to really understand just how these methods can and do work on the structure of your thoughts.

There is no need to suffer at the hands of your own mind with your thoughts or the sounds that play out within the home of your mind. You can take control and you can implement any of the actions outlined previously. You now have these resources to change how you experience life within yourself, for the better. These actions that work are actions that you may be repeating with so little effort and ease, each and every day in your own life with your digital interactions on apps, online, and with the content that you post on social media. As you begin to look at your own personal profile in your own mind, examining the patterns and strategies that you've been running, you can use these techniques demonstrated to help gain more mental and emotional relief and to have better operating choices for the ways in which you use your mind.

Think about it this way: what's better for you in your life – to suffer at the hands of your thoughts, or to take your mind into your own hands? On the surface, you may be able to make it look as though all is well in your world, but on the inside, you may be plagued with the traffic of thoughts that exhaust you physically and emotionally, each and every day. Even if you're playing over the past or feeling anxious through the conversations of panic that are playing through your thoughts on a daily basis, you can now choose to change and transform the interior of the home within your mind. If you're watching the same fearful movies playing over in your head and feeling the same experience of panic in your body that is limiting you from living your life, what are you going to choose? Would you close down the **tabs** with the movie playing? Would you hit **esc** and be free from the content within? Or perhaps you'd **MUTE** the sounds that you hear inside your head? It's your choice to choose to take action. **You can develop more control**.

Implementing these tools as a new system and software update into your own mind and own life can be highly rewarding, but what happens next? For someone who experiences fear and panic or negative self-talk playing through their mind, or negative inner talk to suddenly feel this internal space empty, free, and open, it can feel unusual to remove a pattern that has been in place for so long. As you get used to using your mind and these tools to take control over the things that do not serve you any positive purpose in your life, it is essential that you then develop better programmes, positive filters, and more empowering internal representations that improve all aspects of your life. This will be covered later in the book, so that you can use these new skills to keep the negative out, but you can also then use your mind in ways that allow you to thrive in your life.

I will also share a variety of examples of how to implement these tools and techniques into your life in the next section of this book, so that you can get a real understanding of how and when to use them. Practice and repetition are key, so if you feel you need to re-read this **Digital Mind** section or read and try some of the techniques on your own mindset, allow yourself time now to do so. Having introduced you to these concepts and broken them down for you to refer to, you can try them, repeat them, and allow them to work. As we move forward, you can now gain a deeper understanding of how to improve the home of your mind.

Interlude

Before we move on to re-designing the home of your mind, I want to bring your attention to something really important. Let's take a break and chill for a moment. This isn't a commercial break for me to advertise my services or any other endorsements; it's a break for you to experience just how to **step out of the home of your mind**.

With the tools that I've just introduced you to, which you will be using so unconsciously **each and every day** with your online interactions, you may have tried and tested some and found some relief. By activating your resources and applying them to your mind, you are changing the internal experiences that you are forming in your mind and taking charge to make the content within your mind and your emotions to feel in some ways better. You don't have to **swipe** your way through everything that's on your mind or <u>BLOCK</u> out or **esc** from all that plays out within. In using your resources on your thoughts, you are powerfully becoming more aware of how your mind is working, and most importantly you are realising how you yourself can take control to change and improve things for the better.

In all that I've presented to you, from the very start of 'logging in' to your own personal profile, my intention is for you to become more aware of the thought patterns that run through your mind, and how your mind in itself is set up as a news feed. In your personal reflections of the ways in which your thoughts are being formed on a daily basis, for thoughts that you continue to have over the past or future, your awareness is key for you to make positive changes to your mental and emotional state. With you questioning, reflecting, and observing your thoughts on your inner 'news feed', you are now open to experiencing mental and emotional relief by **using the same actions that you use on your smartphone and apps.** Your awareness of the structure and patterns of your internal world will now be more apparent to you. This is important for one simple and straightforward reason.

From all the observations that you've made about the thoughts that you may watch over, the conversations that ring out loud inside your head, for the fear that you may experience within, you understand that you are always living inside your head. The home of your mind that you transport yourself in for all that you do and for everywhere that you go, is always going to be with you as a constant companion. The walls of your physical home wouldn't be lined with past painful images or conversations playing out loud through your Sonos system, or even your current frustrations played out on your TV screen for you to binge-watch and consume. The environment of the home of your mind that you've occupied for your entire life can now be a place that you tidy up, re-structure, and re-design in order to have a more comfortable and pleasant style of internal living, from the actions that you now implement within. As you use your awareness and as you take action over what's going on within, you can then step out of your mind and arrive mindfully more into the ease of your present space, as you choose to experience more mental and emotional relief.

Mindfulness is a wonderful practice and as Eckhart Tolle said in the title of his best-selling book, *The Power of Now*, there really is so much power in the present moment and so much to gain from **stepping out of the living room of your mind.** As you may have experienced just how to **swipe** or <u>BLOCK</u> someone out of the screen of your mind, or you may have found silence from muting the voice of your boss or husband who just nags on loudly inside your head. Let's experience the power of stepping away from all that draws you in, as you become more mindful of the actions that you can perform with your mind.

Stepping Out Of The Home Of Your Mind

🏠 Simply raise your eyes up from this page and look around you. Notice all that you can in your present environment as your eyes move slowly from place to place. Then focus in on five different objects in your room or environment. Hold your eyes on those objects for 5-10 seconds before you move on to the next.

🏠 Repeat this again, looking at 5 different objects slowly and notice anything else around you, the external sounds, the temperature of the room, the textures, colours, shapes of all that you see.

🏠 What did you notice, observe and experience in yourself?

This is a simple way of mentally 'stepping' into the same space and place as your physical body, and out of the home of your mind. You can be sitting on the sofa at home but mentally back at the office as you re-live the frustration of your colleagues who never turn up for work on Fridays, and **you can also very easily step out of your mind and away from your thoughts.** You may be travelling on a bus physically, yet time travelling through the thoughts in your mind even though the world around you may possibly be a simpler and more pleasant place for you to personally experience, than the contents of your own mind. It's so easy to get sucked into your mind, into the scenes that play over and the conversations that play out loud, yet it's also massively rewarding to **mentally be where your body is.**

As you apply your Digital Mind tools of closing down your **tabs**, **muting** conversations and most importantly pressing **esc**, you will be encouraging yourself to step out of the home of your mind. The more that you experience the ease and freedom of your outer world, the less time you'll want to stay stuck in your inner world, re-watching, re-listening, and re-analysing over and over the news feed of your mind.

 Try it again; look around you. Notice and observe, hear, feel, smell, and sense – all that is around you as you step out of your mind.

It's very normal and natural to think and go from thought to thought. For example, as I practiced the above technique, I observed my orange kettle and remembered the shop it was purchased from. I looked at the bananas in my fruit bowl, and my mind considered what I'd eat for breakfast. As I hear the clock ticking, and feel the cold temperature of the kitchen worktop my arms are leaning on, I am more in my physical home and less in my mental home. **Esc**aping the world within comes through the actions that you choose to execute and the choices that you take to step out of your mind and away from your over active thoughts. In taking more control of what you choose to let happen in your mind, you can, after each action, find further relief by using your senses to be more mentally present and at ease within your physical body. So, encourage yourself to revisit the tools and techniques of your **'Digital Mind'** and persevere in practicing the methods and repeat them often with patience to feel a sense of control and relief inside your mind and your emotions. In each activation that you choose to do, whether you **empty your trash**, **MUTE** any inner sounds, or if you choose to apply **filters** to the faces and voices in your mind, immediately use your senses to <u>step out of the home of your mind</u> and to be more present in your own space.

Keep it simple – get used to activating your power to be present:

 Simply raise your eyes up from this page and look around you. Notice all that you can in your present environment as your eyes move slowly from place to place. Then focus in on five different objects in your room or environment. Hold your eyes on those objects for 5-10 seconds before you move on to the next.

 Repeat this again, looking at 5 different objects slowly and notice anything else around you, the external sounds, the temperature of the room, the textures, colours, shapes of all that you see.

Part III

Exploring The Home Of Your Mind

Chapter 5

The Rooms Inside
The Home Of Your Mind

*The people you surround yourself with will
always influence the behaviour that you have,
as will the thoughts that you choose to keep
company with inside the home of your mind.*

A Moment In My Mind

I wake up each morning and reach for the alarm. As I lie in bed with one eye open – I'm not going to lie – I'm not perfect. My day usually begins looking at emails and hopping between social media accounts on my phone. This brief action then leads me to find personal relief in my bathroom, and there I am brushing my teeth while I am slowly becoming more and more awake. It is pretty much always at this point where I catch my eyes in the mirror and realise, in the space of minutes, I have travelled to so many different places, in so little time, all in the space of my mind. As I look myself in the eye, I find the thoughts of myself replying to client emails, the places I will be driving to that day, the clothes that I am considering wearing, all disappear off into the distance, as I step out of the home of my mind. I then shower, but I'm back in my thoughts, and again I catch myself noticing the water running down the tiles, the steam from my bathroom as I distance myself from my thoughts. It's normal and natural to be consumed in the space within; however, there is no real stress being played out, no negative conversations, and nothing of the sort that I personally need to **swipe** or **esc** from.

This may not be the case for you. From the experiences of those that I've coached and worked with, I've found that, for some, the feelings of anxiety and the thoughts that make those feelings exist in their physical body are active in their mind from the moment they open their eyes. For others, they have even been in and out of sleep from the anxious thoughts that have disturbed their rest in the early hours of the morning. Other people have thoughts of stress regarding children, relationships, and work situations that play over and over to be watched, discussed, and listened in on, all in the home of their mind. These thoughts and situations which feed the feelings are happening at the same time they wash and dress and will continue on the commutes these individuals take as they leave their physical homes, yet travel with their thoughts, in the home of their mind. Their mental homes may already resemble roads of traffic from the continuous flow of thoughts for yesterday, last week, and potentially for later that day, all montaged into the space inside where **tabs** are open, dialogue is being heard, as emotions mix around the body.

🏠 How is the start of your day?

🏠 Where does your mind go to with your thoughts?

🏠 Are you 'open' with various **tabs** or thoughts that belong in the **trash**?

In my personal example of floating between the home of my mind with my thoughts and my physical home, the test then begins. My husband is annoyed that I've rushed him, and I am filled with reasons and frustration that I then want to express, which aren't going to help anybody in this early morning situation. As I drive to my morning clients, the internal dialogue of the conversation I should have had with my husband, fuelled by the annoyance I have towards him, begins to play out in my mind, which I feel in my throat and body as I'm tensely holding the steering wheel. The inner voice is pissed off and loud. My realisations for the beauty of the blossom tree roads that I am so carelessly missing out on brings me to **MUTE** the sounds in my mind – **several times I may add.** I then consciously pay more attention to my drive. I use my eyes to take in the beauty of spring, and my ears are soothed from the tones of Sam Smith playing throughout my drive. The inner voice is now gone; however, the mini-movie begins to play in my mind, which as I drive I simply **STOP** and close down that particular **tab,** and focus on being more present, through my senses. It is the choice of actions that I execute in my mind and my ability to be more present that enables me to feel more mind relief.

I arrive at my client's to find she is not home. She forgot our appointment and tells me that she is on her way. By this time, the beautiful British spring weather has – no surprise – turned to rain, and as I stand on the doorstep shielding myself from the rain, the frustration begins. I think about how I'd be soaked if I run back to my car. I breathe slowly and **swipe** away my annoyed thoughts for her and the situation that I am in, as I enjoy the sound of the rain falling around me – again out of choice. She arrives with a croissant for me and an apology, and any feelings of annoyance have naturally ended up in the **trash**.

Later that day, the sun has returned and I have a podcast interview to prepare for in a break between clients. A message 'pings' on my phone that the delivery I had ordered won't reach me in time and this now dominates my mind and draws me away from the focus of the podcast. I close the mental **tabs** and **MUTE** the inner talk as I **swipe** away the content of my mind so that I can purely focus on the task ahead. This is all in a day's actions of my mind. I choose to focus my attention and to be more mindful of the actions of my mind that are either drawing me into myself and feeding the situation or taking me out of myself and away from my thoughts.

In a completely separate experience, I can remember the thoughts and internal conversations that played over and dominated the home of my mind for me when my mother was taken ill. As I live more than two and a half hours away from my mother, I would often get message updates and calls from my family with regards to the state of her health. Upon visiting her and spending time with her back home, my mother told me directly to go back to my home during her recovery to my work, and to hold things together with the suggestion to visit her at weekends. This difficult period of me being away from my mother as she rested and recovered was a huge torment to my mind, my emotions, to my sleep patterns, and my concentration. I could have lived inside the torment of my mind for hours and days over and over, between the times I was away from her, to the point I sat by her side. In the space and distance between our visits, I had to 'get out' of my thoughts, for the worry was all too consuming. However, it was the thoughts, conversations, and mental movies of fear that were not doing me any favours. It was natural to worry and to be concerned; however, the content of my mind, which feared the worst, played over and over, even though my mother was making a healthy and speedy recovery. As she sat in the hospital laughing with the other patients and telling them jokes and ghost stories, my mind and my thoughts were naturally of fear, panic, anxiety, and worry. It was through my mindfulness approach to **stop** entertaining these thoughts and to **stop** re-playing them and experiencing them in my own head space, that allowed me to find mental and emotional relief as I **esc**aped the montage of constant worry during the time between my visits. **Muting** the worried inner voice, **esc**aping from the fearful content within, closing down the **tabs** of worse-case scenarios were daily actions that I needed to perform to step out of the content of my mental home. There was no point in travelling around the city, with a head full of fear and worry, when back home, and on great authority, I was told of my mother's speedy recovery.

It's very normal and natural to worry, and through practice and repetition, it's also normal and natural to think and then be consumed by the worst possible scenarios that you can possibly think of. However, it was through my awareness and my constant choice of reminding myself that the fear in my mind was simply a figment of my imagination, that I could take action as mentally I was suffering more than my mother was, as she was making a full healthy recovery.

By using the actions and choices that you make and can now make from learning the **Digital Mind** tools that are available for you, you too can reshape and transform the environment that you personally experience within yourself for the better.

The time
that you
spend in
your thoughts
can be empowering
on so many levels.
You do
not need
to live in fear,
assume the
worst,
or stay stuck
in the space of
your thoughts.
You can
very simply
and very
powerfully change,
edit,
and filter the
content of
your mind
for the better,
all out of
choice.

Kamran Bedi

What Lies Within

Have you ever portrayed the perception to the outside world – to those who you spend time with, work with and maybe live with – that all was in perfect order and that from the outside nothing was wrong at all? Perhaps at times you've grinned, smiled happily, and chatted your way through the day when inside the home of your mind you were a complete mental and emotional mess? This may currently be your identity, where you have kept up an appearance of life being superficially perfect and in line with 'what's expected', when within you've been tortured through to your core. You may constantly feel challenged by endless thoughts, tormented by uncomfortable feelings, but all seems well on the outside. For many individuals covering up the pain and not working on the challenges that they experience within can end up having an impact on how life is then lived.

What is the best option to seek help and support for the world that is difficult within? The earlier example of my own anxiety about the Facebook question of **'what's on your mind'** highlights the ways in which we internalise our experiences through thoughts, mental movies, and inner talk, which then leaves us in a particular mental and emotional state. Being in a position to edit, filter, and update the ways of your own mind is now an option that you can work on for yourself for all that **filters** and flows through the news feed of your own mind. Instead of becoming consumed with in-depth internal chatter, and in order to prevent yourself from binge-watching the screens of anxiety, you can use your tools to change and transform the internal patterns that play out in the home of your mind. In working on your environment, the style of thoughts, and the episodes that you watch and listen in on, you can collectively take action to **swipe**, **block**, **filter,** and remove all that serves you no positive purpose in your own head.

As you become accustomed to firstly using your awareness and then taking action to 're-set' the structure of your mind, you can very powerfully remind yourself not to get so consumed by the content and conversations within. Through the actions that you use, you can then choose to be more present as you engage yourself through your senses, to be more mindful, and less caught up in the space of your thoughts.

You can change the ways in which your thoughts operate, and you can use your awareness and tools to execute the same repetitive actions that you do on your external news feeds to change and transform the news feed of your mind. In becoming the architect of your own mind, you can renovate and re-design the style of the personal home of your mind. Let's now look at bringing all of your awareness and all of your tools together as we look now at the variety of rooms that you may often visit in the home of your mind.

The Room Of Anxiety

This is the room in your mind you spend so much time in, where you go over and over and over the possibilities of potential threats, your fears, your concerns, and all that you believe that you potentially have no control over. This room in your mind is covered from wall to wall with open **tabs** of situations that you think up and watch, playing them out over and over in your mind. The sounds of this particular room will be made up of conversations that you have with yourself and others in a frantic, panicked tone and speed that encourages the content that you view to make you feel completely out of control within yourself. Your heart may beat fast, your palms can sweat, and shakes may tremble through your body. Here you are stuck in this room in the home of your mind, binge-watching scene after scene as you project out possibility after possibility, for all that could potentially happen. You fear the worst to come, from the social anxiety of not saying the right thing, not fitting in, not being liked, to a variety of potential threats and dangers that can range from getting trapped in a lift, having a car crash, to even going out in public.

This is the panic room of the home of your mind where **you have pushed the alert button** and switched on all of the internal cameras, screens, sensors, and sounds and this is where you stay stuck in a position watching, listening, feeling, and continually feeding the anxiety from the content that you create and view within.

🏠 Who is coming to rescue you from the panic room?

🏠 Who is going to stop you from viewing the potential threats to your life that plays out over and over in your mind?

The room of anxiety that you may sit in daily or may live in permanently will have far too many **tabs** open, a collective of inner voices and inner conversations dominantly playing out aloud, and a variety of out-dated thoughts and beliefs that have developed in their strength from the time that you've spent in this room in your mind. **Esc**aping and being present is fundamental for you to find relief. **Esc**aping the inner sounds and **muting** them, the screens that are open and playing, and finding relief from the emotions that you feel is vital for your own mental and emotional freedom.

🏠 Who put you in the room of anxiety?

🏠 Who can get you out and away from the experience of being anxious?

🏠 What can you apply to your mind now to free yourself from the room of anxiety that you spend time in within the home of your mind?

esc, **filter**, <u>BLOCK</u>, **STOP**, **MUTE**, **swipe**, **tabs**, and **trash**. <u>Repeat, practice, repeat practice</u> and then take yourself out of the room of anxiety as you *practice being mindful.*

The Room Of Depression

This is the room in your mind where you are stuck in a cycle of thinking and feeling in ways that serve you no positive purpose. The screens within are playing the same stories and same experiences that challenge you mentally and emotionally. The inner chatter that you take part in and listen in on is contributing to you feeling low. This room can feel dark, limited, resourceless, and unhelpful, with little desire or motivation to step out of this room. The door may open many times, but you choose to close the door and shut out the light by drawing the blinds, as the feel of this room captivates you into feeling stuck. It's almost as though your feet are glued to the ground from the emotion that you feel and that makes it feel like a huge effort to rise to your feet, to take any steps, and to change the environment of the space that you sit in within your mind.

How long have you been trapped in this room where you're probably watching over and over content for the past that leaves you feeling locked in this depressive state? The news feed of your mind may well be filled with so many regrets, so many disappointments, and so many thoughts relating to your past. You watch these on repeat as you think of the things that you should have done or said, and you see no way for the future or any hint of the present moment. It is in this room that you are stuck but only in your mind. The space around you in the present moment could free you, if only you can find the ways of your mind that can empower you to step out of this room, to think and feel better, and to now use your mind more powerfully and resourcefully to create a future that has more meaning. Instead of feeling lost in what could have 'once been', you can be free in the present moment. Then you can powerfully use your mind to change and improve the room that you exist in within the space of your thoughts.

🏠 How long have you been in the room of depression?

🏠 Are you stuck in watching and consuming content for what once was?

🏠 Are you able to look past the state of your mind to close the **tabs**, to end the chapters and to change and embrace a new and more positive channel on the screen of your mind?

🏠 What can you apply to your mind now to free yourself from the room of depression within the home of your mind?

esc, **filter**, <u>BLOCK</u>, **STOP**, **MUTE**, **swipe**, **tabs**, and **trash**. <u>Repeat, practice, repeat practice</u> and then take yourself out of the room of depression as you *practice being mindful.*

The Rooms Of The Past, Present, And Future

These are the rooms where you time travel back to what was, what could have been, and perhaps into bouts of depression, and also ahead into the future for what you could positively and negatively create through your thoughts, which can then produce anxiety. The room of being present is a place and a state that is unique and individual to each person. The present place may be a place where you are distracted from the actions that you consume, for when you're scrolling and liking and consuming online content, you will be wondering to the past and future, questioning or creating the context of what you view and how you process that within your mind.

🏠 How often do you experience the full benefits of being present? For when you talk and laugh, drink and eat, walk in nature and for when you spend time doing any activity?

🏠 Are you wondering into different rooms in your mind, or drifting in and out of your present place as you go ahead to what could be, or back to what once was, when in the present moment your ability to be fully free in your mind is then missed?

🏠 Where are you in your mind if you're in the room of the past?

In using your awareness to look at how far back you're time travelling through your thoughts, you can realise that it is through the actions of the thoughts that you are allowing, which are then causing the feelings that you feel as you get distracted for things that are no longer in your present moment. In acknowledging your thoughts, you can then get a sense of what your chosen thoughts from the past are causing you to feel. The simple process of closing down the **tabs** that play over from your past or **muting** the sounds and conversations of what once was will enable you to change and transform how you feel within yourself, all out of choice.

🏠   Where do you go to in the room of your future?

Jumping ahead to the possibilities of what could happen for you and thinking through every potential situation so that you're prepared, ready, and in some ways feeling safe, is going to be exhausting. The effect on your mind and emotions for living ahead for what could be, can also lead to disappointment if you're dreaming ahead for the life that you want and missing out on living in the now. If you're playing content in your mind of difficult situations that could potentially happen, you will be feeling those feelings which probably relate to fear or anxiety, and there you are taking yourself away from the ease and freedom of the present moment. Future projections can simply hold you back from living your life, and most things that you imagine upon the screen of your mind can leave you restricted in the ways that you then live your life. Is it time to empty out the **trash** thoughts that serve you no positive purpose or even <u>BLOCK</u> out the sounds and images that play over and out within that may cause you fear? Maybe the real choice is to **esc** and be present, to be mentally and emotionally free.

The room of the present isn't in your mind – it's in your present, physical space. In the intimate interlude that you experienced after all of the Digital Mind was introduced to you, you had the opportunity to use your senses to be free and fully present. As you see, hear and feel your present place, you can become less consumed in your mind. As you step into the conversations that you're having, the places that you sit and walk in, you can be fully present in your environment and not be playing out potential or past situations in the space of your thoughts. This is a practice that you should encourage yourself to practice daily.

You can now apply any of the methods to your mind to free yourself from the content that takes you forward or back and that may also distract you from being present and free.

esc, **filter**, <u>**BLOCK**</u>, **STOP**, **MUTE**, **swipe**, **tabs**, and **trash**. <u>Repeat, practice, repeat practice</u> and then *practice being mindful.*

There may be many more rooms that feature within the space of your mind that you spend so much time within, watching, projecting, re-visiting and creating, from all of the thoughts that you think and the inner conversations that you have and also listen in on. Using your awareness to see if you're in a room of panic, worry or fear, or if you're in a room of anger, resentment or annoyance can help you to act on the content that dominates the news feed of your mind. You may find yourself in a comparison trap where you cause yourself unpleasant feelings as you compare your life, your relationships, your success, your achievements and all that you are and all that you choose to do, as you compare your life to those who share their content online. In this action of comparing, you may then move quickly from the room of disappointment to the room of regret, or spend time in the room of depression from the content that you allow within yourself.

Conversations that you read in on through text or WhatsApp can leave you having internal conversations or negative tones that lead you into the room of resentment in your mind. Whether you're spending time binge-watching the people in your life in the space of your mind – from friends, colleagues, family or relationships – **you are the viewer and consumer of the emotions and the state that you then personally experience.** Your choice of freedom comes from being more present and in unfollowing the news and contents that you get sucked into, as you choose to edit and update the rooms that you spend time in, in the home of your mind. Nothing in life is going to serve you a more positive purpose than changing and improving the patterns of your mind. As you actively edit and improve the settings that are in place so that you reduce the uncomfortable feelings, you can now enhance the more positive and productive feelings, as you re-discover the power of your own mind.

The Room Of Hope

This room in the home of your mind may be visited less often or depending on your circumstance for yourself, for those you love, or for the position that you find yourself in now in your life, you may spend so much time wishing for a particular hopeful outcome. This is where you have the opportunity to create the space that you want to be in, inside your own mind with your thoughts. This is where you now have the opportunity not only to experience the power of your thoughts and the ways in which you can shape and transform your own internal environment, but it's also an opportunity for you to spend productive time in your mind in forming thoughts that empower the way that you feel, as you fill the news feed within with resources that are more positive.

   What are you hopeful for in your life?

Whether you want to be loved, to have good health, to have a career that fulfils your needs, to travel the world, to overcome any challenges, or to be hopeful for the best possible outcomes in your life, it all starts in your mind. Spending time focussing on all that worries you, all that fills you with fear and dread, all that makes you anxious, or all that stops you from fulfilling the dreams that you desire, **is an unproductive use of your mind.** To have this content playing out on the news feed of your mind

– from thoughts of worry to mental movies of being anxious, even listening to the panicked tones of self-talk that you listen in on – will only harm you and leave you feeling hopeless.

Hope is a state of mind, it is a set of thoughts, images and mental movies, along with positive self-talk that you can build up and engage with through the content that you can create within. To have hope strengthens your ability to believe, and through belief, you can eradicate fear, which can help you to transform the state of your mind and emotions. In building up a room of hope, you are choosing to strengthen the state of your mind and the types of thoughts that are formed within the home of your mind, which will then improve and transform the feelings and emotions that you experience within yourself. The feelings that you feel will feed the thoughts that you think which will then very quickly and very powerfully influence the actions that you choose to take, which will lead to the results that you have in your life.

🏠 Do you need to spend time building up and spending time in the room of hope in your mind?

🏠 How could a simple ten minutes a day of thinking and being hopeful for whatever you need or desire help change how you think and feel inside the home of your mind?

🏠 As you **swipe** and <u>BLOCK</u> out the thoughts that fill you with fear, in choosing to be present, you can also choose now to design and build a room of hope that you can experience in your mind, through your thoughts.

🏠 Spend time now thinking of what you are hopeful for in your life and allow the thoughts to be clear, colourful, bold, and large in size as you watch the mental movies and listen to the sounds of all that you can be hopeful for in your mind.

The Room Of Healing

All healing originates in the mind, starting with the very first thoughts of seeking help and guidance, which leads you to the first action that you choose to begin the process of personal healing. Fear blocks your healing. Consuming thoughts that fill you with worry, and spending time creating anxiety from the thoughts that you allow inside your head, takes you further away from healing. In using your awareness to change the room that your mind spends time in and the types of thoughts that you are engaging in, can allow you to then improve the room that you then think in, as you improve your state of mind. Whatever situation you find yourself in, whether you are overpowered with anxiety, stuck in depression, or hopeless for physical healing, allow yourself time with your thoughts, to eliminate all that disempowers you in your mind. Instead, choose to powerfully transform the way that you think and feel, by spending time with your thoughts, that allows your mind and body to heal.

It may now be clear to you that the mind and body are completely connected, for whatever you think you shall most certainly feel. In realising that the content that flows through the news feed of your mind may be causing your anxiety, and your depression, as well as your mental and emotional pain, you can choose to develop a space within your thoughts that allows you to heal the difficult and turbulent challenges that flow through your mind and body. Thoughts of anxiety require thoughts of clarity. The anxious mind needs to feel secure in your mind and body and to understand that things will be dealt with for you. It also needs to be reminded that spending hours, days weeks and months going over all the potential 'what if's' simply disturbs your peace. Actively feeding and creating thoughts of certainty that you can and will deal with your issues as and when they happen, can contribute to secure feelings that will help bring you to a place of peace. Allow the thoughts of certainty to be confident and reassuring, and encourage yourself through your senses to then step out of your thoughts and into your present space, for with anxiety being future based, you can find healing and ease within the present moment.

Healing depression comes from you pressing **STOP** on the content of your mind that sucks you into the emotional turmoil of the past and being present brings you into the freedom of the now, to be detached from the thoughts that you think and the feelings that you feel. **If you are stuck in your past, you are simply stuck in your mind.** If you can't see past what has happened to you, you are not moving past the thoughts that you allow to fill the screen of your mind. <u>Change your internal channel.</u> Improve what you're watching and allow yourself to move out of the room of depression in your mind. Reducing anxiety and depression comes from you taking action each and every day. Use your awareness to see whether you are stuck in a particular room in your mind and be aware of the content that is on show on the news feed of your mind.

🏠 Use your mind now to think of ten positive possible outcomes, situations and experiences that you would like to have happen over the forthcoming weeks of your life. <u>Do it now!</u>

🏠 Think past any fear. Play out mental movies of the outcomes that you do want to happen in your life, and form more positive and empowering inner talk that allows you to feel better on the inside. <u>Try it now!</u>

🏠 A daily practice in the room of healing where you change and transform the news feed of your mind for the better, can help transform the way that you feel within yourself, all from the actions that you choose to take in your mind. <u>Go there now!</u>

The Room Of Peace

Above anything else in your life developing a sense and space of peace in your mind will always serve you well in ways that you may not now be able to imagine. Let this space be a room, a garden, an estate, a palace, or a temple of peace, for your mind and body deserves to experience the peace that you can create within yourself. If you can experience peace within yourself, then you will see peace in others and in anything that you choose to do. Any internal turmoil that you allow to consume you; if you let anger, annoyance, frustration, or rage fill the news feed of your mind, will flow out in the communication you give to others and also the things that you say to yourself. **Peaceful thoughts powerfully do the same.**

If you do not detach from your work, from the worries of your relationships, the anxieties of your future, or the stress of your present moment, you will allow your mind and body to be consumed by the thoughts that you think and the conversations that you have, which will take you further away from being at peace within yourself. As you fall into a trance of binge-watching the episodes of your life – past, future, and present – all that consumes you will take power over you, leaving you feeling frazzled to the depths of your mind. Peace lies within the present moment and peace is a state of mind that can be created, achieved, and experienced, all from you choosing to <u>BLOCK</u> out the content that distracts you, as you **swipe, STOP** and **filter** anything that disturbs you from being at peace within yourself.

🏠 Is the content of the news feed of your mind often busy, loud or overly dominating?

🏠 Would closing down your inner **tabs**, muting any inner sounds and **esc**aping to the present moment allow you more peace of mind?

🏠 Encourage yourself to have a daily practice of being in the room of peace in your mind so that you can experience this space and place on the inside, to powerfully transform how you feel and live on the inside out.

An Extension Of The Rooms Of Your Mind

Your physical home may be a place of comfort or even a comfortable mess. The mind of your home may feel like a prison where you feel powerless to change and transform the content that consumes you from within. Even if your physical home is perfect and in order, it is the home of your mind that you are always going to spend the most time in throughout your whole life. In exploring the spaces and places that you can go to in your mind and in changing and updating the content that flows through your internal news feed, you can change and improve the state of your mind and your emotions in any place and in any space that you choose to perform an internal renovation. There are no limits to the spaces and places that you can go to in your mind that allow you to feel and experience positive and uplifting thoughts and emotions. In the same ways that you can be stuck in the dark rooms of depression and doubt, you can actively lift yourself up off the sofas of those rooms and walk into another space in your mind. This comes down to you mentally taking action and making the choices to move yourself through your thoughts and through your choices to then have better internal experiences for the rooms that you sit with inside your mind.

Allow yourself to think of the types of rooms you would like to design in the space of your mind, in your private and personal internal space. What kind of rooms do you think the children in your life have inside their minds? The room of adventure? The room of unicorns? The room of fun and happiness?

By staying stuck in the rooms of your mind that leave you feeling stuck in your life, you not only block yourself from feeling positive emotions but also from gaining resourceful solutions. **Your mind is your greatest asset.** When used correctly and positively, you can find powerful solutions and create wonderful experiences. This cannot be achieved by sitting in rooms of your mind that leave you simply stuck. In becoming aware that the room of love, or the room of joy is going to make you feel better because you only have loving and joyous thoughts in those internal spaces, you need to make time to make sure those spaces exist within. The rooms of your mind will constantly be revolving, and it is through your choices of taking action that you can change and improve the type of home that you live in inside your head.

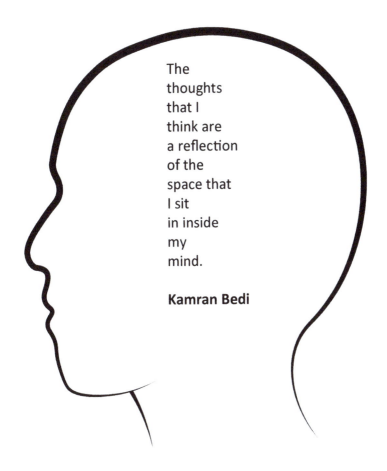

The
thoughts
that I
think are
a reflection
of the
space that
I sit
in inside
my
mind.

Kamran Bedi

For Sale

Where would you want to live?

House one has five bedrooms, two bathrooms, two living rooms, off street parking, and is located on a beautiful road. The interior is in need of work unfortunately from years of neglect. The rooms are very dark with lots of layered wallpapers which are outdated and peeling off the surface. The heating works when it wants to, and the environment can often feel cold and damp, but you can get used to that. Some of the pipes tend to leak, although wet floors and puddles to walk through may be a new interior style trend. The electrics need re-working; however, if you can physically put up with the odd electric shock here and there, and live through the pain, it's not a major problem. The garden is fully overgrown with most of the shrubs and overgrown weeds blocking any light from coming into the back of the house. The landscape of overgrown chaotic darkness feels very uncomfortable to step out into. The layers of dust will leave you constantly sneezing and the toilet flush is broken. This property is a real charm for those who like to live in uncomfortable places or those, who like to feel overwhelmed and tend to let things get on top of them. The current owner says, *'feeling uncomfortable is comfortable, it's just something you get used to putting up with'.* This five-bedroom decrepit property comes with a garage full of random clutter and trash, as the current owner, a confessed hoarder, has trouble letting go of what's not needed.

🏠 Is this the environment you want to live in?

House two also has five bedrooms, two bathrooms, two living rooms, off street parking, and is also located on a beautiful road. An alarming difference here – and you should be warned – is that this property has an immaculate interior. This may seem very uncomfortable for some people. The rooms are perfectly tidy, with lots of light coming in through the large, open windows. The house flows beautifully from room to room and can feel like quite the sanctuary from its neutral tones and comfortable fabrics, making the environment within inviting. Everything is in perfect working order, so this is not suitable for those who like problems, challenges, and things going wrong. The garden is very private and has elements of a Japanese Zen garden – where you should be warned –it is very easy to relax in this beautifully landscaped setting. Taking this property will require very little work, and will require you to live easily and peacefully, with lots of empty and open storage spaces to fill up with beautiful and resourceful personal treasures.

🏠 Is this the environment you want to live in?

🏠 Do you appreciate the sarcasm or metaphor?

🏠 Were you affected subtly or directly?

🏠 Can you see clearly the home of your mind?

There is no right or wrong way to live. There is no perfect life, apart from the filtered Instagram version that you may find yourself comparing yourself to time and time again. Life will be challenging as well as rewarding and you will have easy times and difficult times, times of happiness to times of frustration, through your whole life journey. In all that you experience, you can choose to find peace and freedom from the way in which your mind structures the experiences that you have. You can choose to be in a position where you are not a prisoner to the thoughts that you think and experience, as you become the creator of the changes that you can so very easily execute within your mind. In updating the settings of your mind, you can repaint and redecorate the space that you experience within as you take a position where you take action to make transformational improvements to the home of your mind.

Mentally think about the home in your mind and how it appears in its environment, the mood that you experience within, and the activities that you engage in with your thoughts.

🏠 What do you notice?

🏠 What do you see?

🏠 What could you change and improve?

🏠 Who have you let into your personal space?

🏠 What needs removing or updating?

Allow yourself to reflect and to take action within the space that you experience so personally and so often within yourself.

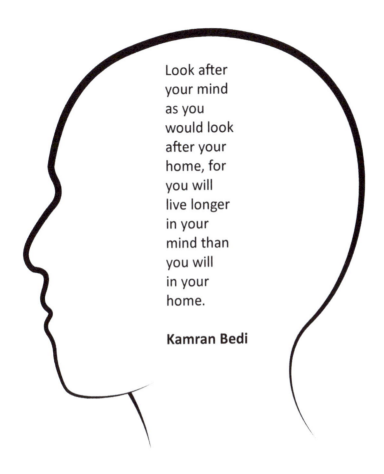

Look after
your mind
as you
would look
after your
home, for
you will
live longer
in your
mind than
you will
in your
home.

Kamran Bedi

Part IV

Moving Into The

New Home Of Your Mind

Chapter 6

Action Leads To Results

Each day you will find you either heal the things that need healing in your life, or you allow them to continue as they are.

Questions For Reflection

Can you recall a time where you continuously drove around a roundabout for hours on end, choosing to stay stuck going around in circles? Perhaps you let your washing machine at home leak out water and just stood and watched it happen? I bet you've had that specific time where you cut yourself, and instead of applying a plaster to the blood, you just let it run freely – no panic, no concern – you just hoped for the best? I'm guessing that none of this has happened in your life, and that you would have acted on all of these; to fix, to care for, and to heal all that you could possibly control in your life?

What about the state of your mind? Have you let your problems dominate the screen within, or have you taken action to make things easier or better for yourself? Have you carried around relentless mental torture and pain? Or have you used your mind for your highest good?

It can seem so normal and natural to stop the floods happening in your physical home, to paint over and fix the cracks, and to weed out, prune and perfect your garden at home. It can be natural and of priority to turn the heat on to feel warm, to open a window to get some fresh air, and to set the lighting around you to improve the mood and environment that you sit in, but what about the mind that you live in? Even if you're sat comfortably on your sofa with perfectly chosen fabrics and colours, the environment within the walls of your mind may be far from at ease. Physical comfort may be yours, yet mental exhaustion may be the experience that you're having on the inside. This, however doesn't need to be the case.

In reflecting on the thoughts and situations that you may be struggling with, and with the mental and emotional distractions that are exhausting to spend time with, you can come to a more comfortable position through simply questioning the state of your mind. Very simply look at and listen to the contents of your mind and all that flows through the news feed of your thoughts. Consider what you are binge-watching, listening to, and being a prime viewer of, and notice most importantly the feelings that you are experiencing in your physical body. In your observations and your findings, notice if the content that only you can observe is stopping you from living your life. Notice the effect it is having on your life, your relationships, your interactions in life, and all that you can simply yet powerfully observe, and then ask yourself one simple question:

Does this belong in my mind?

Whether you are faced with anxiety about the prospects of future travel, the stress of your relationship, the worry about your children at school, or if the past is more present in your mind, or the future is dominating your present moment, simply stop and ask yourself, *'Does this belong in my mind?'*

Being aware is a choice you can make that is going to relieve you of hours of mental torture, or even days or weeks of watching the same fearful scenes play over and over on the screen you watch within. It is always going to be through your awareness of what is happening on the inside, that you can come to a position to change things for the better.

'Does this belong in my mind?' – Question yourself and the actions of your mind, to simply heighten your awareness and to change and improve your mental and emotional state.

In the comfort of your own home, surrounded by your own personal possessions, see yourself sat comfortably watching the content of your mind on your own television screen. As you observe yourself sitting and watching the screen in your home, imagine the walls of your living room decorated with the words used in the self-talk you engage in or the panic, worry, or negative chatter, written clearly on the walls of the living room of your home.

What would you see and be watching? What would you read from the words that flow through your mind? What would others experience if they stepped into the living room of your mind? Just take a few moments to reflect on this scenario where your inner world is wallpapered in the words are conversations that fill your mind.

Having now cleared your internal screen from what you imagined, think about what belongs in the **trash**, what sounds need **muting**, what **tabs** need closing, and what scenes you need to **esc** from. It is your awareness that is the key to you unlocking yourself from the rooms that you feel stuck in and live in within your mind, and it is your awareness that can lead you to use the skills presented to you, to now arrive in a more comfortable and pleasant personal environment within.

Next time you're looking at your phone, your laptop or tablet screen, be it at home or work, imagine the content of your mind reflecting back to you on the screen that you look at. What would you see playing out, or what would you hear? What would be there for others to also view and see? Would you choose to close it down or change the channel or would you sit for long periods of time, re-watching and re-experiencing the content that is projected out?

If it wouldn't make it on to your online news feed, then it doesn't belong in your mind. If you wouldn't want to share it with the world, why allow yourself to become consumed with the content that overpowers you from within? If you feel powerless to the thoughts and conversations within, you can simply and powerfully use the skills on offer to help you find more mental and emotional relief, by changing the content of the screen within. It is in your choice of taking action to have more control, that can lead you through your awareness to then be less in your mind and more in the freedom of the present moment around you.

No matter where you are in your life, what country you're in or travelling to, what company you're keeping, whether you're surrounded by friends or alone, **you are always going to be in the company of your own thoughts**. People may come and go in your life, jobs may change, things may get worse or better at any point in your life, but you will always have the company of your mind and the space within your own head, each and every day.

Inner Temple Or Inner Torture

In repeating the actions to change and improve your mindset on a daily basis where you use your awareness to stop overthinking and over feeling, to stop re-analysing and re-playing, you can form new mental habits that change and improve the home of your mind. Anything that you give time and repetition to becomes a normal and natural habit. You've put the time and effort in to so many different things in your life, each and every day to get the things that you need working for you and working to their full potential. Use this opportunity now to work on and to develop your own mind and your thoughts. You did not know how to work your smartphone instantly, yet you would have persevered to get it working for you. You may have taken driving lessons and sat your driving test, to be able to transport yourself through free choice to the places you want and need to get to. You may have trained for years through investment of time, energy, finances and effort to certify in a specific or a variety of skills that enables you to now be employed and to be of service, and you may still be studying or learning as you develop your craft.

Because of all the learning and developing that you've done in your life, and from all the time and effort that you've put into getting to the place where you currently are in your life, you are now in the position to allow yourself to grow further personally.

This opportunity is for you to develop yourself now, to learn how to have more control of whom you are and how your mind is working. The control that you can learn and now experience can help you to renovate the environment that you experience within yourself, as you very quickly come to learn just how to operate your mind.

You can now free yourself from the days of self-torture, which may have felt at times like you had no control of the content that filled your mind. For those times that you've sat at the mercy of the characters and scenes that played out on the screen within, you now have the opportunity to change your mind and how it is functioning with great ease. The days of self-viewing as you watched over the problems and challenges within your mind and to listening to the possible destructive negative inner talk can now be a thing of your past, through the actions that you now choose to apply to your thoughts. **It all comes down to you choosing to take action – and most importantly – actually taking action.**

Can you think of one person in your life, or even one person in the media who you look up to? Someone who appears to have it all, confidence, a great positive attitude; someone who is living their life the way you would perhaps like to? How do you think they think? What thoughts do you think they have going through their head and what's your role model's inner talk like?

What do you think the environment of their home is like inside their head?

Nobody has the perfect mind with their thoughts, and we all have to deal with our own challenges in our own times during our life. However, it is the 'dealing' with and 'coping' that others may do well with ease that you too can now implement to your own mind and your thoughts. In leaving behind the thoughts that do not positively serve you, in **filtering** the tone of the inner voice that tells you you're no good, or even better **muting** it, you have the opportunity to then re-design the home of your mind to the style and satisfaction of your choice.

Your inner world can be an inner temple. Your mind can be a garden of clarity. Your space with your thoughts can feel like a slow walk across the most beautiful beach – all from you choosing to act upon the methods that you currently have on offer to you. Developing the space that you walk in, think in, spend time in, and live in can be achieved when you **filter** out and update the programs and patterns of thinking that you may currently have in place. Peaceful thinking will lead to peaceful living, which is something that you can definitely achieve for yourself with your mind and in your life.

A point that I'd like to make clear to you, is that the challenges of your mind that you've faced in your life or may currently be facing, whether they include over active thoughts, low self-esteem, anxiety, panic, depression, or fear are common patterns of thinking experienced by individuals all over the world. Other people, including those who you know experience the same private and personal experiences that challenge you and that may be all too familiar to you. It's very easy to apply a natural filter of smiling on the outside and to be falling apart on the inside. It's also very easy for you to implement more mind awareness and control. The point I am raising here with you, and that which I feel is an important message to highlight and to share, is that your loved ones, your siblings, your children, your friends, and colleagues will all at some point in their lives have challenges of the mind. Those challenges that you have experienced may have unnecessarily been with you for years in the home of your mind. You may have mentally suffered and emotionally crumbled from years of spending time in your mind with these difficult thoughts. In learning and experiencing the shifts that you can create for yourself, you can also understand that others – including those you love – can also experience the positive shifts that you experience in your mind and in your life.

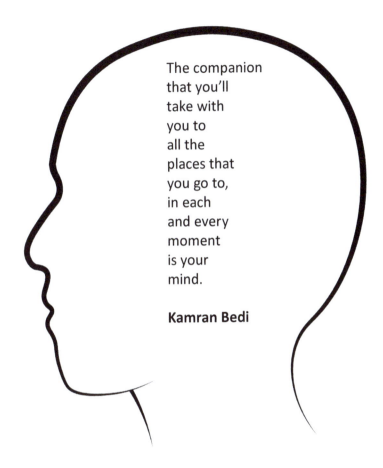

The companion
that you'll
take with
you to
all the
places that
you go to,
in each
and every
moment
is your
mind.

Kamran Bedi

Clearing Your Internal Hard Drive

The content of your head can actually feel like family, friends and in some strange ways, company. You may have carried around, memories, characters, personal grudges and past pains for so long that when edited and updated can suddenly leave you with a wide-open space within the home of your mind. Then what!?

One particular lady I worked with had lived with anxiety for over twenty years. Twenty long years of wondering various 'what if' situations over and over and also questions of 'how will I cope', thought after thought, image after image, inner chatter that held her captive in her mind and in her life. This particular lady was really held captive in her own head, by the actions that she allowed, the scenes and dialogues that played repeatedly, and the content that she scrolled through daily, on the news feed of her mind. Even though she had difficulty doing certain things like going to particular places, or being around certain people – even travelling – she found huge relief from gaining access to the user manual of her mind. We worked together on Skype, so that she was in the comfort of her own home, and we applied some of the process you've just been through to change, edit, and update the content that consumed her from within. *'I've never felt such relief'*, she informed me, with tears running down her face. *'It feels so peaceful within my head'*.

This was a normal day for me, showing individuals how to stop doing anxiety, and showing them the actions in their mind that are causing them to feel distressed. Days passed with thank you messages coming in. The peace had lasted, and she was implementing the actions on the screen within, leaving her more in control, with more self-awareness and more mental and emotional relief. It didn't surprise me when the message came through on my inbox, 'Can we schedule another appointment please, the sooner the better'? Instead of fretting over what she now needed or questioning if the techniques had fallen apart, I muted any negative inner dialogue of worry and <u>BLOCKED</u> out any images of her telling me that this hadn't worked or lasted and got on with my day. Her appointment came back around, and it was with no surprise that the start of her session, the intention of her call was to discover just 'how to live'. *'I feel at peace, I have more control, but I have lived with those symptoms for so many long years, I don't now know what to do with myself'.*

When you come to a point where you have control over the anxiety – the stress and fear that plays on your mind – you can feel as though you are being presented with a blank canvas, an empty road, or a journey that you do not know how to move forward on. Peace can be powerful. Mental ease can feel rewarding. However, the patterns that were in place can potentially leave you feeling like a void in their place.

Imagine, if you can, how light your arms would feel from putting down two 1.5 litre bottles of water that you'd held on to and carried around for twenty years. Imagine how much lighter your back and shoulders would feel if you took off a rucksack of heavy stones that you carried around with you each and every day. **Imagine, right now, how much lighter your mind would feel if everything that troubled you and all that consumed you was suddenly out of sight.** You wouldn't carry around anything in your arms or on your back for a whole single day. The tiresome feeling on your physical body and the mental strain of holding on would taunt you and test you to the point of exhaustion. Make no excuse for yourself for the weight that you carry in your mind, for you have the power within yourself, to put down the heavy content that bashes away at your inner self, to free yourself from the shackles of your mind of the weights that cripple your emotions.

'He said' is a weight that you can let go of. 'She did' is a burden that you can free yourself from. 'They made me feel' is a scene that you can remove from your mind and empty into your **trash**, for anything that causes your mind to feel heavy does not belong in the home of your mind.

The wide open and free space that you can create in your mind leaves you to redecorate the interior of the space that you live in within. You get to arrive at a place where you can step out of your mind to feel and be as free in each present moment. The option of changing the content on your inner news feed to show more positive and empowering news is yours then to filter into and post into the news feed within. You have the power to stop any self-harm, and now the opportunity to create an inner world that you can shape and influence and which you can come to love.

It is often clear to me from the people who I work with that the more positive and uplifting experiences tend to not be posted and viewed as often in the news feed of their mind. It can take real effort to locate, to access, and to view those happy and uplifting times on their inner screens, especially if the content within has been a regular slide show of problems and challenges. It can, however, be achieved. It can be created, filtered, played, and heard, all of the positive, the happy and the joyous inside the home of your mind. Through whatever effort it takes, the energy that you put into spending time within with all that harmed you, can now be brought together for all that can positively serve you, as you actively re-create an empowering space within your own head.

For me, accessing the memory of getting engaged on a white sandy beach, under the stars with the overwhelming feelings of love and joy is accessible in under a second. I only have to mentally think of the beach and the memory explodes over my screen within, which I have stretched out to the size of a billboard, and intensified the colour, clarity and content and allowed it to play at normal 'regular time' as if I am back there within a second. This is what you too can do with your mind. As you begin to edit and eliminate all that bothers you, you can access past memories that evoke a positive state or create future situations that help move your life forward. It's your mind, your internal news feed. As you edit and update the content that flows through the news feed of your mind, allow yourself time to use the same similar actions to then feature and focus upon all the good that you possibly can. Let's now look at how you can powerfully improve your mind having made the edits and updates from your Digital Mind tools.

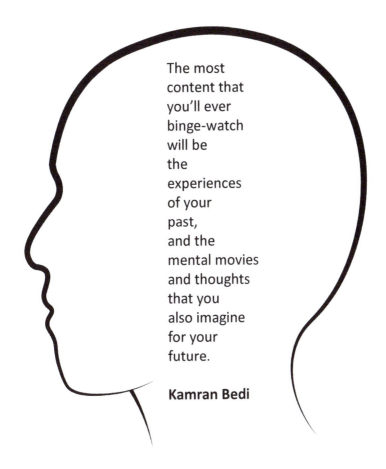

The most
content that
you'll ever
binge-watch
will be
the
experiences
of your
past,
and the
mental movies
and thoughts
that you
also imagine
for your
future.

Kamran Bedi

Chapter 7

Accessing The Unlimited Power Of Your Mind

If you can think of every worst-case scenario, then you can also think of every best-case scenario.

Swipe, Edit, Mute And Then What?

After you first learn how to filter an Instagram post, record a story for Facebook or WhatsApp, your general digital actions very quickly become your new normal. If you think back to your determination to get your phone up and running when you set it up, or when you put the time and effort into your Tinder or Grindr profile to make it as perfect as you possibly could, you simply put the effort in. Putting the same time and effort into your Digital Mind to work with the content that sits in the home of your mind can allow you to take and have more self-control. But what happens when you rapidly change the content within and step into the freedom of the present moment as your ability to be more mindful gets easier and easier? Then what?

What do you do in your physical home to relax and in relation to your general use of time?

You probably spend a lot of your time scrolling on your phone; watching Netflix, YouTube and various other TV programmes; listening to music and spending time with those you enjoy the company of. You are generally choosing what you consume and what actions you view, and part take in. The next step for you in using your mind to your highest good after having made a rapid action using your Digital Mind and having stepped into the present moment, is now utilising your skills for more positive mind actions.

Let's get straight to the point.

Open Positive Tabs

As you close down the overwhelming, busy, and anxiety inducing **tabs** in your mind, you can choose to have more positive internal representations that you have open and playing in the home of your mind. Simply try it now.

1.

Think of a place that you've been to that allows you to feel calm, relaxed, and at ease. Take yourself back to a place where you felt life was easy for you and see this memory – this stilled image or mental movie – vivid, colourful and clear on the **tabs** you open in your mind. Take your time and try building this image and memory now. Make the internal representation that you see clear, colourful and large in your mind. Spend time now building up this memory and positive place in your mind and notice how you feel.

2.

Do the same in another **tab** for someone you truly love. See the person clearly in the space of your mind and spend time thinking of all of the things that you love and cherish about this person. Allow any other positive memories to fill up the **tabs** you can actively open in your mind. Try this now.

In closing down the difficult and overwhelming mind **tabs** you have open on the screen within, you have not only the choice to be more present and more mindful but to also change the channel and the **tabs** open within, to more positive and empowering screens that improve how you feel. This all comes from you taking action, using your mind, and choosing to take control.

3.

Another approach for you to implement into your day-to-day actions is for every time you choose to close a **tab** for the work situation that's playing over in your mind, or for the anxieties you have about your relationship, is to open up and replace it with a positive **tab**. The more positive content that you have flowing through the news feed of your mind, the more positive feelings you are going to experience within. In building up more normal and natural habits with more positive content instead of binge-watching the channels of fear and worry in your mind, you will very quickly and very naturally come to find your mind works for you and not against you.

Encourage yourself each day to have positive still images of yourself and others as well as positive mental movies playing through the news feed of your mind. As you close down the **tabs** that bother you, choose to open up and consume **tabs** in your mind where the content improves how you feel.

Turn The Volume Up

When you hear a tune on Spotify that you love, or when you're driving, and you just want to sing along, you grab the volume and turn it up. In doing so you increase the personal experience and heighten your sense of and association with the music that you listen to. As you actively **MUTE** the voice of self-doubt, the internal conversations in your head that's telling you your friends are bitching about you, or the voice of anxiety that causes you to panic breathe; you can make all of that change quickly through **MUTE**. Choosing then to listen to the silence in your head, the sounds around you as you become more mindful is freeing, but you can turn the volume up inside your head for the inner talk and sounds you <u>do</u> want to hear. It's as easy as you taking control.

My advice to you is to find the voice in your head that is confident, the voice that is positive, the voice that isn't full of panic, and turn their volumes up. It can take time to locate the voices and to bring up their volumes, but in the same way as you effortlessly **MUTE** sounds on your phone on a daily basis and turn the volume up to really hear the content of the posts and videos that you want to hear, you can actively take action on the sounds inside the home of your mind.

How does this help you? Well, it improves the sounds that you listen in on and it gives you the opportunity to change and improve your beliefs. If you lack self-confidence and if you feel that you are stuck believing the views of others who have overpowered and dominated the home of your mind, you now have the opportunity to turn down the sounds and voices inside your head and to turn up the sounds, voices and inner talk that improves your life for the better. You will have a collection of different voices that will be located in different locations on the map within your mind. Some voices will be in hiding, some will be overly powerful, some won't dare to talk now that you're looking for them.

In working with inner voices, sounds, and internal conversations – both positive and negative – with clients over the years, I've found it's always a joy to find those voices that 'used to be there'. The positive voices at times may have gone into hiding from the fears that have dominated the space within, overpowering the voices that want you to live your best life. So, as you **MUTE** your way through the negative, destructive, and unhelpful inner sounds, you can spend time each day in strengthening the type of inner talk, the beliefs and most importantly the volume to feel a sense of personal power and more joy for the playlists that you stream inside the home of your mind.

Stop But Also Press Play

Pressing **STOP** as you use the remote control of your mind allows you to take stock of what's continually looping around inside your head. It is through the **STOP** action that you can always go to another Digital Mind action to edit and update the news feed of your mind so that you feel more control and more relief. As you activate **STOP** on those mental movies that play out and the sounds and conversations within, it's always a great point for you to then step into the present moment to use your senses to see, hear, and feel your personal space.

It's also a great opportunity for you to form new positive habits to **STOP** the action that's bothering you and to **press play** on the complete opposite action, to train your mind to overpower the worst-case scenarios that you view with so much ease. For every time you find yourself watching those mental movies of self-doubt where you're not good enough, not confident enough, or when you find yourself being self-critical and stuck in a rut of self-sabotage, press **STOP**. Having pressed **STOP** and having found relief and then the choice of being more present in your current place, you can press play on a variety of images and mental movies that powerfully light you up on the inside.

In using your mind to visualise and to improve your personal inner talk, immediately play scenes of you being more confident in your head and encourage more positive self-talk. Play and see images of you being good enough in the areas of your life that you want to feel good, for what you choose to think you will always feel, and you will always act from the way that you think and feel. Try it now. Begin to see yourself in your mind and see all the positive qualities about yourself. Hear yourself internally praising yourself and notice the effort it requires for these scenes and sounds to play. Investing your mind and time in playing this type of content for yourself and about yourself will help fine tune your mind to embrace more positive self-love. In improving the news feed of your mind with content that supports you, you can allow yourself to grow from the time that you invest in your mind with your thoughts, to change and improve your state of mind for the better.

Make it a daily practice to **STOP** fear and to press play on your dreams. Press **STOP** on your anxieties and press play on being in the present moment. Press **STOP** on the voice that tells you you're not worthy and press play on the voice that says every part of you is wonderful. Press **STOP** on what harms you and press play on all that empowers you, each and every day.

Fill Yourself Up With Filters

In a click of a button online, you can literally transform yourself into a unicorn covered in glitter. You can also **filter** your voice and give yourself a whole comical identity from changing the way that you are represented on a screen. In the same way you use the **filter** function of the Digital Mind to find relief for the people that overly dominate you inside your head, dressing them with bunny ears and shrinking them down into Lego-sized figures, you can also **filter** the whole of the home of your mind. Mentally, with your thoughts you do not have to be stuck in the pain and darkness of your mind. If you can change your digital screens, you can transform the screen within by filtering the style, the environment, the brightness, and the focus to improve the set-up of the home in your mind.

Practice using **filters** to realise how you can change your thoughts for the better.

1.

Think now of a good friend and as the person pops up in your mind dress him or her up as a unicorn inside your mind. **Try it now** and see how applying a filter in your mind to that person changes how they appear in your mind, and also how their image makes you feel. **Do it now.**

2.

Think back to an old school teacher and shrink him or her down in size. **Do it now** and notice how you can use your mind to shrink them down in size.

3.

Transform the image of an ex in your mind to that of a horse face with a horse's voice and notice how the person now makes you feel. **Try it now.** How different is it for you when you think of them now with this filter? **Do it now** and see and feel what happens.

Instead of being dominated by other people in your mind and being consumed with emotions that you find difficult to digest, **change the recipe** of the structure of the people and the places in your head by **filtering** them to feel more comfortable within yourself. Changing other people's voices that you hear in the home of your mind and even putting them on **MUTE** can also provide you with instant relief. Using these daily actions is going to help you understand the power that you have to change and improve the content that you consume within, as you activate your Digital Mind.

Breaking Free

Escaping the content of your mind couldn't be easier and moving from the rooms that fill you with fear is only ever a single thought away. How often have you had repetitive thoughts that just play over and over, thinking and feeling the same thing over again causing you to even lose sleep? Anxious thoughts tend to loop around in your head. Depressive thoughts tend to be a narrative and montage of thoughts that leave you feeling low and stuck from moving your life forward. Instead of being overly consumed by what is going on inside of you, you can freely choose to **esc**, (and use your thumb and finger as a button as described in the process earlier), to remind you to step out of the room that you're stuck in with your thoughts.

Do not allow yourself to feel lost in the room of confusion. Encourage yourself to break free of the room of emotional pain. Press **esc**ape and choose to be mindful. **Train your mind** for each time that you find yourself stuck in a room that doesn't serve you, to then move yourself to a room that improves your state of mind.

The room of gratitude should exist in your mind. You can design it in whichever way you desire but let your whole body be filed with joy as you turn your inner light on and as you actively feel the joy that your mind can create by simply counting your blessings.

Try it now. Think of ten things in your life that you feel grateful for. It could be the people you love, the place you live, the things that you've experienced and achieved. What can you feel and express gratitude for now? **Try it now.**

Sitting in the room of gratitude in the home of your mind each and every day will train your mind to find blessings in all that you experience. In choosing to think in a space of appreciation, you can very easily and quickly eradicate any negative feelings or difficult thoughts as you train your mind to focus on what is good in your life. Spend at least five minutes each day – if not longer – in the room of gratitude in the home of your mind. Instead of being kept awake at night from being in the room of fear, you can fall asleep in a state of joy by choosing to sleep in the room of gratitude in the home of your mind each and every night.

Blowing Your Own Trumpet

There's no better way to clean up the desktop of your mind than by emptying out the files, beliefs, self-made mp3's of self-doubt and self-sabotage and emptying out your personal **trash**. Some of the thoughts and beliefs that you have in place may have your internal hard drive space unable to take in any more data. You may feel tired and heavy from all that you're storing within and choosing to empty out your internal **trash** can allow you to feel relief in various areas of your life.

As you grab, drag, swipe, and drop the people, the memories, and the beliefs down into your personal **trash**, you can choose to fill your newly found space with positive qualities about yourself. Self-validation, self-love, self-worth, and self-esteem are all so much better than self-sabotage. As you edit and move the content and items that no longer serve you positively in your mind, you can choose to be more mindful and to feel more present. You can also empower the screen and space you personally view within.

🏠 How often have you told yourself you're worthy or that you're doing a great job in trying to keep your life together?

🏠 How often have you praised your efforts or even reflected on your own personal achievements?

I have coached so many people with confidence issues who have achieved so much personal success in their lives, but they never seem to bring up past achievements on the news feeds of their minds.

Allow yourself to be proud of who and how you are. Even if the biggest achievement this month was you getting yourself up off the sofa and moving out of the room of depression in your mind, praise yourself. If you're a parent constantly giving to your kids, praise yourself. If you're achieving great results at work, praise yourself. Praise yourself now for at least five things that you've achieved, accomplished, started, or attempted this month and value your personal efforts. **Do it now.**

Stop sitting in the room of 'things could be better' and fill your screen and news feed in your mind with positive images and mental movies of all of the positive things that you are. Have no more self-doubt, no more 'I'm not good enough'. Take time each day to praise who and how you are, and especially in the times you choose to empty out your personal **trash**.

Your Ultimate Timeline

Probably the most important news feed in your life is the one that sits inside your head, the one that only you know, the one that only you can personally work with and change yourself, for yourself. The time you spend going from each social media timeline, scrolling and liking, interacting, commenting, and passing judgment as you filter and edit the reality of what is, to gain satisfaction from the likes and comments that you get from others, is in comparison less important than the content you view inside your own head. It all comes down to you. Allow yourself the time and knowledge to work with the content that you view, that consumes you, that you enjoy – and also perhaps detest – inside your own head. Encourage yourself to work with the tools that you use so effortlessly each and every day on your social devices to help you to cope with the world that you experience within. Stop being an inactive observer who just watches in on the content that fills your inner timeline, and choose to be more active in reshaping, and controlling the news feed of your mind.

You may have had mental movies that play the same scenes over and over on repeat. You may feel the pain of the content that you view, and you may feel powerless to change, stop, or prevent the scenes that dominate the theatre of your mind. Whether its emotional pain, anger, or anxiety, the news feed in your head doesn't have to be a trance of repetitive and uncontrollable distress that you feel unable to stop and control. Whether you find yourself stuck in the room of anxiety, or if you feel there's no light within from sitting in the room of depression, the doorway to the room of hope is always there.

⌂ What is it that you need to shift with your internal viewing to consume a better news feed inside your head?

As you use your awareness to change and to transform, to make your personal news feed within more bearable for you to live with, your life can rapidly change for the better. It all comes down to you being aware of what you're allowing to fill the space within the home of your mind, and then you taking action on the content that's inside your own head.

⌂ Would you allow a negative, aggressive saboteur to step into your living room to sit in the corner and talk to you in ways that are destructive?

⌂ Would you sit in the living room of your physical home and watch the same fifteen seconds of your life where you were hurt by someone else over and over on repeat on a TV screen?

⌂ Would you search the internet for every possible worst-case scenario that could happen to you in your life, spending hours viewing and feeling the worry from the content that you consume?

If you wouldn't allow it to enter or to have the time and space in your physical home, then do not ever allow it to take over the home of your mind.

Remember that it is your awareness that is going to help you break the cycle that leads you to then use your Digital Mind actions to find relief within. In being aware, remind yourself often to ask the question, *'Does this belong in my mind?'*

Utilising and installing the Digital Mind within yourself to edit, to change, and to update your personal settings for how you internally represent the content of the news feed of your mind, will allow you to find peace within yourself that will filter into all areas of your life. As you begin to feel the benefits, as you choose to take action and to gain control, you will feel the power shift as you **mute**, **swipe**, **filter** or **block** all that you choose to edit from the screen within. In using your actions and in stepping into the ease of being more present and less online in your mind, you will also notice the helpless actions of those around you who are stuck in the position of viewing and not acting over the news feed of their own minds. This is your opportunity to close down those **tabs** and mental movies that fill you with fear, as you begin to give the same amount of time and energy you give to your smartphone, to now working on the home of your mind.

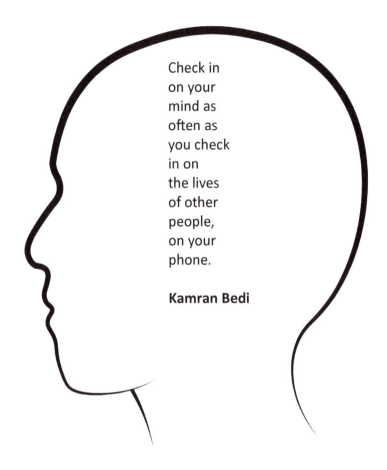

Check in
on your
mind as
often as
you check
in on
the lives
of other
people,
on your
phone.

Kamran Bedi

Part V

Transforming Your Internal World

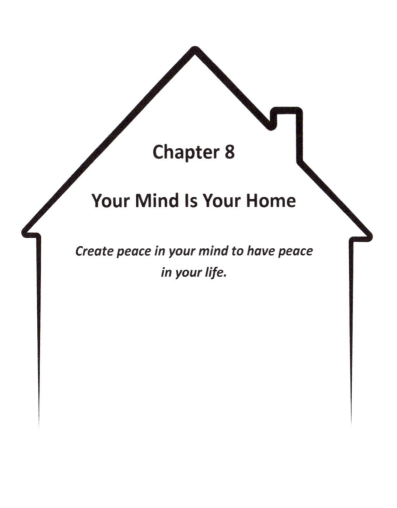

Chapter 8

Your Mind Is Your Home

Create peace in your mind to have peace in your life.

Your Mental Health Matters

Making a hair appointment for a cut, colour, or blow dry just seems to happen so naturally and for some with great emphasis on maintaining the perfect set of locks. Getting a flat tyre on your bike or car is normally fixed immediately, for I'm certain that you wouldn't continue through life at a slower pace. Even a burst water pipe in your home can call for immediate action and attention so that your comfortable home doesn't get water damage. What do you do when you have a problem with your mind, though? From the people I've had initial consultations with to the people I've coached, there is a general resistance to taking action on improving one's mental health.

🏠 How often do you work on your mind?

🏠 How often do you see a professional therapist, practitioner, or coach to help you with your mental and emotional health?

🏠 How often do you implement the tools and resources from the hundreds of self-help books that are written by experienced professionals that can help you improve your life?

🏠 Do you spend endless time stuck in the problems of your mind and not investing in the possible solutions?

When are you going to take action?

The Digital Mind that I have covered in this book will help you to act quickly to find immediate relief for how you are internalising and processing your experiences in your life on the news feed of your mind. You will need to repeat some actions until you feel the difference you want to feel. You will need to combine some of the practices together, perhaps three or four methods – or even all of the skills – to help you to feel comfort in the home of your mind. Some will last, and some will need reactivating. Your ability to be more mindful and less consumed by your thoughts will also need action on a daily basis in order for you to re-programme and re-wire the patterns of your mind.

I'm almost certain that you can type a text very quickly at times, and sometimes without even paying any attention to the screen of your phone or laptop. This wasn't mastered in a day. If you think back to learning how to drive or even ride a bike, the time put into learning new ways allowed you to develop new skills and to move your life to a place where you could transport yourself around. It's the same with learning a new language, a new sport or skill, and it's the same in learning how to use a new social media app. You learn, you practice, and you put the time in. This is the same requirement for you to work on now, to take control of the state of your mind and the content that you allow to play out within. This is important for the simple reason that **your mental health matters.** Summer bodies don't transform overnight. Learning to meditate doesn't get mastered in an hour. The only thing that might guarantee a next day result is an Amazon Prime order. If you want to improve your mental health, if you want to think and feel better, and if you want to live more comfortably in the home of your mind, **you have to take action** today, tomorrow, and for the rest of your life.

As a leading practitioner, I often hear endless excuses. I hear people who are in mental and emotional pain but are unwilling to do the work and to invest their time and energy in healing themselves. The two most common phrases that I hear from the people that I work with are: *'I just want to feel like myself again'* and secondly '<u>I wish I had acted sooner</u>'**.**

I've worked with people who have suffered within for over twenty years, who have found relief in a single ninety-minute session. That's twenty years of not travelling, feeling scared and having a news feed that fills them internally with fear. Taking action to develop a mind that you can live with will allow you to change and transform your mind for the better as you come to be in a position for knowing just how you can cope.

These methods that I present to you are to help you to take effective control of the issues that challenge and overly consume you, so that you can find instant relief. In the therapeutic and coaching world, there is often a deeper issue or narrative that is underlying in the individual that causes conflict and discomfort in the home of the mind. This isn't the case for everyone, but primarily for some. The resources I present to you may offer you permanent relief as well as the awareness and knowledge that you can be in a position to help and improve your own mental and emotional health. They may offer short-term relief on the surface. For the deeper parts, you may need a more thorough intervention, but do not give up on yourself as it is you and only you who can take action, seek assistance, and help yourself heal.

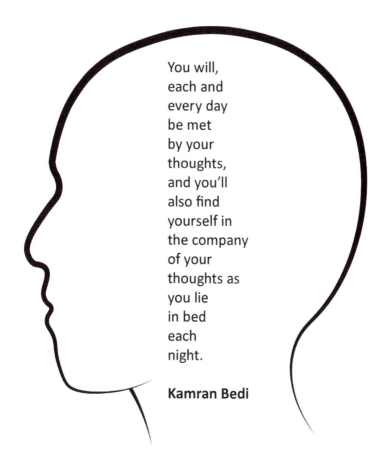

You will,
each and
every day
be met
by your
thoughts,
and you'll
also find
yourself in
the company
of your
thoughts as
you lie
in bed
each
night.

Kamran Bedi

What Do I Need To Do?

I had been interacting with followers through questions around mental health on my coaching Instagram account @coachkamranbedi. I do often encourage a mindful approach through my online account, to be more present in your real life and to use your Digital Mind to bridge the walkway towards the ease of the present moment and away from your difficult thoughts. One question, in particular, gave me a huge realisation. I was asked, 'Does the book, Mindfulness, work?'. This led me to answer quite briefly because of the limitations of text that fit an iPhone screen, but here is my extended answer:

From personal experience, I know mindfulness does work. I've actively taken action myself on a daily basis to being mindful in a variety of ways, from the conversations that I have, the places that I drive through, the music that I listen to, the nature I walk in, the food that I eat – I actively choose to be mindful of and not distant in my thoughts. Mindfulness works. The simple act of noticing my breathing, being with my breath and not in my thoughts, and consciously extending my breath to be longer, slower, and deeper again allows me to be more mindful and less distracted from my thoughts. The work I do with my clients allows me to be mindfully present for the one-to-one experiences I share, and the practitioner trainings that I deliver also allow me to be more mindful of myself and my students. Mindfulness works.

The Digital Mind works to change and to edit the people in your head, the fear that you binge-watch, the relentless self-doubt you talk yourself through, as you can very easily **swipe** it, **filter** it, **mute** it or **block** it. These interventions work, **only if you do the work.**

My simple response to the Instagram question was: it's not so much about whether the book works. With all self-help books, **you the reader, have to do the work.**

Allow yourself to find relief by putting the time and effort in on a daily basis so that you can take control of your mind and your emotions, because your mental health matters. Remind yourself that you are not alone in thinking the way that you think and feeling the way that you feel, as everyone goes through feelings of anxiety, stress, worry and fear at various points of their lives. In my experience as a coach, again I see numbers of people who want help but don't take action and then the suffering only continues. Getting help doesn't mean that you are weak, it doesn't mean that you can't cope; it means that you realise the importance of your own mental wellbeing. The ways in which you may struggle with your thoughts are also the same ways that others may struggle with their thoughts, for the experiences that challenge them in their life. Allow yourself to realise that you too can change and improve your own mental and emotional wellbeing by choosing to take action, for those who you love and care for, may also, at times, have difficulties living in the home of their minds. In your understanding of how you can transform your mind and emotions for the better, and from the dedication, time, and effort that you put into the home of your mind, you could one day help those that you love, after you've spent time helping yourself.

Building A Home For Your Mind To Live In

I have asked you so many different questions throughout this book to encourage you to step into your own personal inner world and to look from a different point of view, perhaps, for the ways in which you are using your mind. Questions allow you to reflect, to search, and to expand the way your personal situation is structured and viewed within. It is through questioning that you can potentially find different answers, angles, resources and solutions that can lead you to take personal action.

My direct and immediate – if not blunt – question at the start of the book asked you to consider, 'What would you be left with if you practically lost everything?' This question wasn't to make you think about a disaster in your life, but to make you realise that you are what you think you are, and life is based on the labels and titles that you define life by through your thoughts and beliefs. So, choose not to reflect on all that you would lose, but more on what **you could actually gain**, for you may in some degree lose the objects, people, and values that you attach to those items; however, **you will always have your mind.** Life will always be a journey each and every day through highs and lows, love and sorrow. Everybody feels and everybody thinks, but not everybody finds ways for how to cope.

In understanding that you can use your mind to help you reduce the pain and suffering and to increase the love and joy that you feel within, you can understand that you can use your mind as and when needed to help you experience the shifts that you desire in your life. Whether your mind is strong or weak, developed or lacking in its ability to see any possible solutions for what challenges you, you will never be immune from the life experiences that we all collectively go through at different points in our lives. What is powerful for you and what can potentially change and improve the experiences that you do have within comes from you actively understanding and then utilising the environment that you choose to freely change, edit, and update, that I presented to you as the home of your mind. If you find that it is your mind that you want to lose for the pain and suffering that you feel and experience within your thoughts, choose instead to lose the current ways of your mind, as you choose to renovate and restructure the home that you live in inside your own head.

You may not be in a position to change and update your physical home, but you are now in a position to change and transform the home of your mind. A simple **five minutes a day** can allow you to practice being mindful and less in the space of your thoughts, and even in that valuable five minutes, you can close down any **tabs**, **MUTE** any internal chatter, and make good use of the Digital Mind tools. In the same five minutes or at any point you choose, you can realise which room you are in inside the home of your mind, simply from the way that you are feeling. These daily actions of training your mind to build up mental strength can encourage you to then use these skills, awareness, and tools as and when needed throughout your day. It is with your commitment to your mind and your thoughts, that you can commit to your own mental health as you build a comfortable home for your mind to live in. This travelling companion that you wake up in, move your life around in, and fall asleep in is always going to be in your presence for all that you do and for everywhere that you go. Allowing yourself to have more comfort in the space that you are going to spend the most of your time in your life, comes from you choosing to take action to design and build an internal environment that is of personal comfort for you. For all the people, situations, dilemmas, challenges, and issues that walk into the home of your mind, you have the power and the opportunity to welcome in those guests, or you have the power to **show them the door,** as you actively use your awareness and your now Digital Mind. It is always through practice and repetition that anything you put your mind to becomes a normal and natural habit. This goes positively and negatively, so if you continue to talk the talk of self-doubt, or if you allow yourself to nervously dance to the erratic tune of anxiety, that is what is going to be normal and natural for you. Developing new ways of thinking and embracing new ways of living comes from you and the choices you choose to make. The cost of you tidying up the home of your mind, to re-design and to re-build a space that serves you positively, mentally and emotionally is of no charge; it simply takes time.

If you can learn how to use a smartphone, how to move and navigate through a new dating app and how to **filter** and edit the information that you post online, then you can very easily learn and embrace how to edit and reshape the content that flows through your mind. It always comes down to your choice. For every time you change a TV channel, you can use the same actions with the channels of your mind. For every time you **swipe** a piece of content away on your smartphone, close a **tab**, **MUTE** an annoying video, BLOCK a cold caller or follower, you can implement these actions on the news feed of your own mind. As you apply **filters** to the selfies that you take, you can **filter** the people and situations that play out in your thoughts. For every time you pick up and use your smartphone, you will be reminded to use the actions of your Digital Mind within the home of your mind, on the world of your thoughts that you personally experience within.

To feel better, you need to direct your mind to work in ways that serve you better. To live better you need to act out of choice. May your journey into renovating, building, and designing the home of your mind be even more pleasing and rewarding as the number of likes you can muster from the people online who you do not know. Remind yourself that the one main follower that you have in your life – the one main person who can give you the biggest 'like' – **is yourself,** and that will always start and end in the **home of your mind.**

Disclaimer 2

Never have we been in a time where your mental health is constantly influenced by the activities we seemingly unconsciously take part in, each and every day. As a nation, we have moved so quickly through the last ten years with the development of technology and the ways in which we've changed how we communicate. This leads me to stress the point that it is of great importance to update the way that you communicate with yourself. My offering to you is to be aware of the content of your mind, and the time you spend binge-watching and over consuming the content of your own internal news feed. In bringing together the Digital Mind, aligned with the day-to-day actions that you know all too well, you can find personal relief by you choosing to take action for yourself, and on yourself.

The Digital Mind is my own interpretation designed to help you, the reader understand and to work with the content of your mind in ways and with actions that you can very easily relate to. The modalities that I use personally with clients that I coach from severe anxiety, depression, PTSD, insomnia, fear, personal and business coaching come from the skillsets that I am certified and experienced in including; NLP, IEMT, Hypnotherapy, Timeline Therapy and Mindfulness. In a session with me, you can expect to have a variety of modalities used on you from my repertoire of skills. From my initial understanding of NLP for how the mind works, I have been influenced to design a new way of working with the mind, that which I present to you and also use successfully with clients: this is the Digital Mind. I look forward to developing this method further and for you to integrate it into all areas of your life, from what I offer to you in this book, for you to now implement into your daily life.

For more information on my coaching services or for first-hand assistance to help you with the home of your mind, please visit kamranbedi.com or for daily motivation you can find me on Instagram @ coachkamranbedi

Installing A New Mindset

I invite you now to embark on a 21-day programme utilising the Digital Mind as you install it into your daily life. In coming into a position of taking action with your mind and with your day-to-day challenges, you can utilise the Digital Mind techniques not only to take control of the news feed of your mind, but to also practice being more mindful. The more that you work with the content that flows within the timeline of your thoughts the more control you are going to have over the way that you feel and the way that you then live. You can start on any day that you choose. Just spend a minimum of five minutes a day closing down **tabs**, **muting** inner sounds, and **filtering** the content in your head that can lead to you having more normal and natural responses and in you taking charge over the content that consumes you from within. Begin by being aware of your thoughts and by taking action as and when needed to help you have more mental and emotional control of your mind. Then remind yourself to choose to be, and to also practice being more mindful and less in the space of your thoughts, throughout each day.

Here is a recap of how to step out of the home of your mind and how to be more present. Practice this daily.

Mindfulness Recap

🏠 Simply raise your eyes up from this page and look around you. Notice all that you can in your present environment. As your eyes move slowly from place to place, stop on five different objects in your room or environment. Hold your eyes on those objects for 5-10 seconds before you move on to the next.

🏠 Repeat this again slowly on five more objects in your environment and notice anything else around you – the external sounds, the temperature of the room, the textures, colours, shapes of all you see.

🏠 What did you notice, observe and experience in yourself?

As you read the final section of this book, you will now have further insights about how, when, and where to apply the Digital Mind practices with examples including; anxiety, stress, negative inner voices, painful past experiences, and more…

I also invite you to get an online experience with me understanding and being coached through the Digital Mind on my online programmes over at kamranbedi.com

For daily motivation you can find me on Instagram @coachkamranbedi

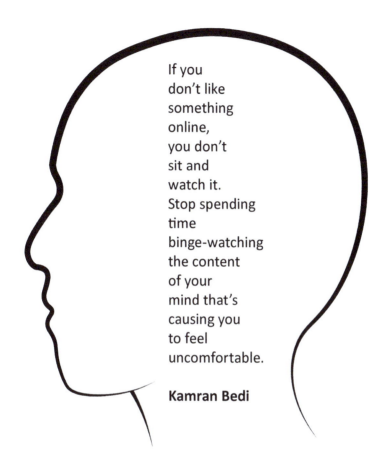

If you
don't like
something
online,
you don't
sit and
watch it.
Stop spending
time
binge-watching
the content
of your
mind that's
causing you
to feel
uncomfortable.

Kamran Bedi

How To Apply The Digital Mind

This section gives you further insights and examples of situations that you may be challenged with in your life. You can apply the suggested methods or use the Digital Mind techniques in your own way and for your own challenges, as well as choosing to be more mindful to help improve the news feed of your mind. Remember that a minimum **five minutes a day** of using the Digital Mind can make a huge positive difference in your life. With each example you can choose one action and one option or considering if necessary, using more than one action and one option.

<u>Anxiety</u>

Notice what is on the news feed of your mind. Are you seeing still images and/or playing mental movies or scenes in your head? Do you have any internal chatter or internal voices that are talking fast, loud or anxiously in your mind? Are you sitting in the room of anxiety in your mind, surrounded by anxious thoughts and sounds?

Action - Press **STOP** on the scenes and images playing inside your head and press **MUTE** on any inner sounds. Repeat this process if necessary.

Action – **Filter** the content of your thoughts. People – turn them into smaller sizes with floppy dog ears. Situations – **filter** the screen in your mind until it is completely bright white to wash out the situation playing in your head that's causing you to feel anxious.

Option – Be more mindful and less inside your head space with your thoughts. Use your senses to step fully into your present space as you step out of your mind.

Option – Step out of the room of anxiety and step into the room of calm. Create a space inside your mind that is peaceful and tranquil. Really build up the environment and make it vivid and real so that you mentally spend five-to-ten minutes a day in this calm room of the home of your mind so that you can step into this space anytime you find yourself in the room of anxiety.

<u>Stress</u>

What is causing you to choose to feel stressed? What is the situation? Who is the person or people causing you to choose to feel stressed mentally and emotionally? Once you highlight the person, people, or situation and how you may be choosing stress as a response, look at how it presents itself on the news feed of your mind. Are you replaying the situation over and over? Are you talking through every situation in your mind that could go wrong in your mind, or analysing over and over the things that have already happened and caused you stress? Is it a reoccurring situation in your life that is dominating the news feed of your mind?

Action – Close the **tabs** that are open in your mind. Check in on how many tabs are open and draining your mental and emotional battery of your mind and body. Actively close the **tabs** down.

Action – Press **esc** on your thoughts and choose to be more mindful and more present so that you are less consumed with your thoughts. Repeat this action to encourage your mind to step out of your thoughts.

Option – Step out of the room of stress in the home of your mind. Make the environment inside your head lighter and brighter by bringing up more positive thoughts, scenes and mental movies to move your mind away from thinking and consuming stress. Open the windows to the room you move into in your mind as you breathe in deeply, exhaling slowly to reduce the stress you feel for ten minutes, while you sit in a more comfortable space in your mind. If any thoughts pop in, **swipe** them away.

Option – Be more mindful and less inside your head space with your thoughts. Use your senses to step fully into your present space as you step out of your mind.

<u>Overthinking</u>

Are you giving too much airtime to the thoughts inside your head? How is overthinking your situation of every possible outcome helping you at this present moment? Are you sitting on the sofa but running a marathon in your mind? Feeling exhausted? Binge-watching your thoughts for what was, what could happen, and what could go wrong is only going to add weight to your mind.

Action – **STOP** scrolling through the news feed of your mind. **STOP** thinking through every situation and **STOP** thinking about what others involved will do, feel, say, or think. Press **STOP** over and over again.

Action – Empty your mind of the thoughts that need placing in the **trash.** Drag and drop them away from your mind and the present moment, and make them disappear from the screen of your mind.

Option – Change the channel inside your head as you sit in the room of gratitude. **STOP** yourself from overthinking as you choose to feel good from counting your blessings. Spend ten minutes in the room of gratitude and encourage your ability to feel grateful to grow and expand.

Option – Physically do more. **STOP** overthinking and participate in an activity that requires your attention. Use your mind and your awareness to be more mindful of what you are actually doing as you reduce the time you spend scrolling through your mind.

Taking things personally

'He's thinking', 'They believe', 'She doesn't care' – are you reading into things that you don't actually know are true? How many WhatsApp messages are you interpreting negatively, thinking you know what other people are thinking or saying about you? What are you saying to yourself inside your head? What are you overthinking and then over feeling as you choose to believe what you perceive to be true?

Action – **MUTE** all inner talk/discussions/other people's voices/beliefs/perceptions that may be making noise inside your head, causing you to feel uncomfortable. Find peace from turning the sounds off and keeping them off inside your head.

Action – <u>BLOCK</u> out the content that dominates the news feed of your mind. **Swipe** it away off your internal screen, off into the distance and stop playing the game of 'I know what they are thinking and saying about me'.

Option – Open up a single large **tab** on the screen of your mind and play out ten positive qualities you can think of for the people involved. Play out ten positive memories or future situations that reduce your feelings of being victimised as you actively choose to feel good within.

Option – **Filter** the people involved who you are choosing to see as individuals who are directing negative energy toward you. Filter them into freeze frame images with floppy dog ears. Make them as cute and as innocent as possible in your mind by changing the tone of their voice and making them seem and sound as cute as possible.

<u>Negative inner voice</u>

Whether it's your voice that's giving you negative chat or someone else's that won't get out of your head, use your awareness and notice what kind of things are being said inside your head. Is it overly loud? What is the tone? How many voices are there? Can you even locate the voice/voices or are they switching from one to another or moving around? Hunt them down with your awareness and take action.

Action – Press and firmly hold **MUTE** on the voice or voices that serve you no positive purpose in your mind.

Action – If it's someone else's voice that won't go away, turn their voice into a toddler's voice that is high pitched, very slow and very slurred as you **filter** their voice.

Option – Spend time each and every day finding your positive voices, whether that's confident, motivated, self-belief, self-power – whatever is positive and productive for you and turn the volume up of these voices as you **MUTE** all negative voices.

Option – Change the playlist of topics and conversations that are playing through the sound system of your mind. For every negative and destructive inner conversation or sentence said by someone else inside your head, **MUTE** it and hear out ten positive sentences/statements/beliefs/ to override the negative inner voice. Do this every time and every day to re-train your mind to be more positive.

Difficult past experiences

Are you often visited by past experiences in your mind that cause you to feel particularly difficult emotions? Perhaps the past is something that has dominated the news feed of your mind that you can't seem to escape from?

Action - Close the **tabs** that are open in your mind. Check in on how many tabs are open and that are draining your mental and emotional battery of your body. Actively close the **tabs** down.

Action – Press **STOP** on the scenes and images playing inside your head and press **MUTE** on any inner sounds. Repeat this process if necessary.

Option – Be more mindful and less inside your head space with your thoughts. Use your senses to step fully into your present space as you step out of your mind.

Option – Move yourself out of the room of your past that you may be stuck in inside your head. Move yourself into a room of the present and allow yourself to build up the ability to be less in your mind with your thoughts as you choose the present moment over any thoughts of the past. Encourage your inner voice and inner screen to close down any **tabs** that pop up or **swipe** them away as you actively take control of your mind.

Ex relationships

Whether your ex has moved on and you're still stuck stalking the images of 'what was' inside the news feed of your mind, or you're replaying mental movies of the relationship you once had, and future projections that the person will be yours again, choose now to take action on the content of your mind.

Action – **Swipe** the person from the screen of your mind. Repeat this and keep your ex out of mind and out of sight.

Action – **Filter** your ex's face whether you choose positive or negative, **filter** him into a frog and eliminate the image of him being a prince that's stuck in your head. **Filter** his voice to that of a cartoon character, **filter** the appeal out of them inside your mind.

Option – Turn your intentions to the future and enjoy the present moment. Build up your self-worth and self-power by increasing the volume of the voice inside your head that knows it's time for you to let go.

Option – Be more mindful and less inside your head space with your thoughts. Stop time travelling back or forward and thinking of him, use your Digital Mind to **swipe** him away and to be fully in the now.

Health

Ongoing health challenges can take their toll on the home of your mind. Feeling frustrated, angry, and fearful can leave you experiencing a cocktail of emotions that you find difficult to stomach. By using your awareness, it is important that you build up a room or rooms inside your mind where you can rest your thoughts so that you can allow your physical and emotional body time and space to be free of the thoughts that may add further to your discomfort. As you seek medical advice and care, a daily active utilisation of using your mind can help you find mental and emotional relief.

Action – Place your fears and worries in the **trash**. **BLOCK** out all of the negative and fearful projections in your mind and close down the busy, noisy, and over active tabs that are draining your energy.

Action – **Swipe** away the thoughts of worry along with any thoughts of panic, worry, fear or stress. Allow your mind to be a positive place that allows your body to feel more positive and empowering feelings.

Option – Create a room of inner peace where you spend time in your mind in the comfort of your thoughts as you open tabs of thoughts and mental movies with a projection of positive health. Develop an outlook with the outcome you desire and use this outlook as a reference point to remind you to feel at peace in your mind and body.

Option - Be more mindful and less inside your head space with your thoughts. Use your senses to step fully into your present space as you step out of your mind.

Emotional abuse

Whether emotional abuse is a thing of the past or a current challenge that you face from people in your life who are causing you to feel emotional discomfort, a daily practice of spending time in your mind to validate yourself and re-establish foundations of self-worth can allow you to find more comfort in the home of your mind.

Action – **Mute** the inner sounds/voices/conversations that you may hear inside your head or that may play on repeat. Silence those views, words, or thoughts and experience the peace you can feel within.

Action – **Swipe** away the faces and internal representations that may seem overly dominant in your mind. Shrink them down to tiny Lego-sized figures as you **filter** their appearance and **mute** their voice.

Sleep problems

An over active mind is never pleasant to deal with as you close your eyes and attempt to sleep. It's like watching the cinema screen of your mind play over and over every situation. As you talk through and listen in on every voice having pillow talks and late-night chats in the space of your mind, you find yourself walking like a zombie the next day from the lack of beauty sleep you're getting.

Action – Close the **tabs** that are open in your mind. Close down all screens, movies, thoughts that are playing and presenting themselves at this inappropriate time as you lie trying to sleep.

Action – **Mute** the conversations and sounds inside your head and hear only silence. Hear only silence. Hear only silence!

Option – Take your awareness to the feeling of your pillow as you mindfully lie in the space that you are in and choose not to lie in the content of your mind. Choose to create a room of sleep in your mind that you walk into and lie down in where you can't be disturbed by any thoughts.

Option – Use your senses to feel the bed beneath you – the comfort that you lie in – and very slowly scan through your body starting with each toe. Moving through your toes, slowly sense and be mindful of the feeling of your duvet, sheets, and bedding on each part of your body as you relax your mind further and further to fall naturally into a sweet sleep.

<u>Fear</u>

The panic room in the home of your mind may have alarms ringing for all that you fear from the content that flows through the news feed on your screen within. How is the panic that you watch, listen in on, and play a character in holding you back in your life? Are you feeling stuck from what you're consuming inside your head? Can you see how you're a prime viewer to the movie and soundtrack playing inside your mind?

Action - **Stop** scrolling through the news feed of your mind. **Stop** thinking through every situation and **stop** thinking about all of the things that could go wrong. Press **stop** over and over again.

Action – <u>BLOCK</u> out the images and movies that play in your mind having pressed **stop,** apply a <u>BLOCK</u> screen to cover any panic or fearful thoughts that are playing through your head.

Option – Immediately move out of the panic room of your thoughts. Take yourself to a more comfortable place and space by choosing to be more mindful of your physical surroundings and less inside your mind.

Option – Open a **tab** in your mind to have positive and reassuring situations and scenarios play out on the screen within so that you get used to focussing on the best-case scenarios.

Confidence

Notice what is on the news feed of your mind. What's happening within to make you feel unconfident? Are you seeing still images and/or playing mental movies or scenes in your head? Do you have any internal chatter or internal voices that are talking fast, loud or anxiously in your mind? Are you sitting in the room of anxiety in your mind, surrounded by anxious thoughts and sounds?

Action - Press **stop** on the scenes and images playing inside your head and press **mute** on any inner sounds. Repeat this process if necessary.

Action – **Swipe** away all negative and unconfident scenes you see in your head and all representations that you have of yourself that you feel are not confident.

Option – Allow yourself to play more confident and positive inner talk about how you represent yourself or for a situation that you want to be more confident in. Take time to let this voice and scenes be seen and heard and keep any unconfident views and inner sounds closed down and on mute.

Option – Place all beliefs that leave you feeling unconfident in the trash as you drag and drop them out of your mind to clear up new space for better internal representations.

<u>Depression</u>

What room are you sitting in in the mind of your home? Are you venturing back into the past for what was and not letting go of the things you can no longer change? What's dominating the news feed of your mind that's causing you to feel stuck?

Action – **Swipe** away the thoughts of worry along with any thoughts of panic, worry, fear, or stress. Allow your mind to be a positive place that allows your body to feel more positive and empowering feelings.

Action – **Mute** all inner talk/discussions/other people's voices/beliefs/perceptions that may be making noise inside your head, causing you to feel uncomfortable. Find peace from turning the sounds off and keeping them off inside your head.

Option – Move out of the room of depression in the home of your mind and move yourself into a more comfortable place that improves how you feel with your thoughts and feelings.

Option – Be more mindful and more present in your space and surroundings to stop venturing off to the past for the things that you can no longer change. Take action each day to be more present and more productive with your thoughts and daily actions.

Comparisons

Are you spending too much time online on social media, and looking at other people's 'highlights' that are causing you to feel anxiety, stress, and elements of not being good or perfect enough from comparing your life, your relationship, or job to other people?

Action – **Stop** bringing the things that you see online into the news feed of your mind where you then binge-watch the content of your thoughts. **Esc**ape and be more mindful and less stuck between the news feeds of your phone and the news feeds of your mind.

Action – **Mute** any internal chatter that's causing you to feel inadequate. Drag all content in your mind that doesn't make you feel good within into the **trash**.

Option – Change the channel inside your head as you sit in the room of gratitude and **stop** yourself from comparing your life to other people's as you choose to feel good from counting your blessings. Spend ten minutes in the room of gratitude and encourage your ability to feel grateful to grow and expand.

Option – Be more mindful and less inside your head space with your thoughts. **Stop** time travelling back or forward and thinking of them, use your Digital Mind to **swipe** them away and to be fully in the now.

Your opportunity
to work
on the
mind that
you live
in and
the thoughts
that you
keep company
with that
influences
how you
feel within
yourself is
available to
you each day
for the
rest of your
life to create
more peace
and comfort
in the
home of
your mind.

Kamran Bedi

Acknowledgments

I would firstly like to express complete gratitude to my patient and understanding husband David, who has not only supported me in all that I do but has kindly sacrificed so much time in allowing me to work on producing this book. I am truly grateful for your never-ending support.

Special thanks and endless love to my dear friend Katie Piper for providing the foreword and for continually encouraging me with my message in assisting others with their mental and emotional health. I am truly grateful for your friendship and support and I thank you for the years of supporting me online in sharing my content and posts to your wide audience.

Debra Tammer, I thank you for kindly encouraging me to write, for taking time to look over my work and for always supporting me and encouraging me for everything that I do. Thank you! Miri Freud for always being a beaming ray of sunshine and a voice of encouragement, thank you.

Extended thanks to Mauro Murgia for your endless help and assistance in being my photographer!

Special thanks to Jessica shuffle Kainth for repeatedly 'trying out' the scripted and step-by-step sections of the Digital Mind in helping me develop this method further.

Huge love and thanks to Mr Sean Patrick, my publisher, writing coach and mentor for this book for allowing me to have my voice, my style and my way for writing the book the way I wanted. Thank you for motivating me and assisting me in getting this far.

Special thanks to Dan Schaffer for years of mentoring, business ideas and the 23 formula.

Appreciation to all my clients past and present for the years of learning and developing that I have personally done as a practitioner and for the insights that I have gained in helping you move forward with your minds and also your lives.

Thanks to my loving parents, family and friends, for the time I sacrificed with my head staring at my manuscript.

Extended thanks to Micheal Downing, Keeley Dann, Vicki Savini, Peter Watkins, Jonathan Jones and Katie Brockhurst.

Connect with Kamran Bedi

Kamran Bedi is an international wellbeing practitioner, motivational speaker and mental health advocate who works with people all over the world on improving their mental and emotional health.

You can connect with Kamran online and also receive daily motivation, join a workshop, training or an online course. For all services and connections, please visit:

Instagram @coachkamranbedi

Twitter @kamranbedi

Facebook.com/kamran.bedi

kamranbedi.com

mindbodymethod.co.uk